THIRD EDITION

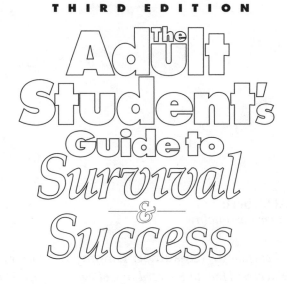

The Adult Student's Guide to Survival & Success

also by Al Siebert:
The Survivor Personality

Peaking Out

Learning Psychology, (co-author: Timothy L. Walter)

Student Success: How to Succeed in College and Still Have Time for Your Friends (co-author: Timothy L. Walter)

also by Bernadine Gilpin:
Career Cycles

Teaching College Success to Older Students, instructor's manual to accompany *The Adult Student's Guide to Survival and Success*

College Survival and Success, a student's manual to accompany *The Adult Student's Guide to Survival and Success*

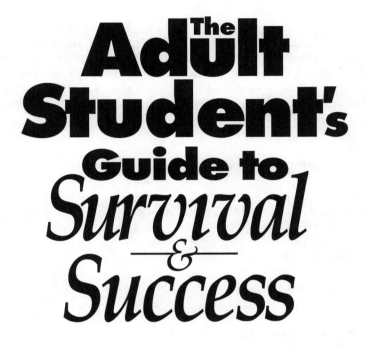

THIRD EDITION

The Adult Student's Guide to *Survival & Success*

AL SIEBERT & BERNADINE GILPIN

Contributing editor:
Samuel Kimball, University of North Florida

Foreword and comments by Mary Karr

Practical Psychology Press • Portland, Oregon

Practical Psychology Press
P.O. Box 535
Portland, Oregon 97207

Book design/prepress by Kristin Pintarich
Illustration by Teresa Rosen
Cover design by Robert Steven Pawlak
Printed with soy ink by Thomson-Shore, Inc.

10 9 8 7 6 5 4 3 2 1

Publisher's Cataloging in Publication
(Prepared by Quality Books Inc.)

Siebert, Al.
    The adult student's guide to survival & success / Al Siebert & Bernadine Gilpin ; contributing editor, Samuel Kimball ; foreword and comments by Mary Karr. -- 3rd ed.
    192 p.   cm.
    Includes bibliographical references and index.
    Library of Congress Catalog Card Number: 96-70010
    ISBN 0-944227-12-0

    1. College student orientation--United States. 2. Study skills.
I. Gilpin, Bernadine. II. Title.

LB2343.32.S54 1996   378.1'9
                                      QBI96-40211

Contents

To all students
with the courage and commitment
to pursue their dreams

Foreword

I did it! I graduated from college with honors and I've now completed a graduate degree. ME! With a husband, four children, three dogs, a cat, and a 44-mile commute each day.

Do you feel nervous? Wonder if you will be able to study and pass tests? Concerned about the effect that your going to college will have on your family or friends? Worried that your car may break down or have a flat tire one morning? Feel like you won't fit in? If so, then you know how all the rest of us felt when we first started!

The Adult Student's Guide will help you deal with all your concerns and more. It has the kind of practical information that usually comes only through experience. It shows how to develop effective study habits and good test-taking skills. It has lots of information about how to get through the institutional maze, information that can help you avoid the costly time and money mistakes that can frustrate anyone.

Mainly I would say that if you believe in yourself, and take things one day at a time, you can get the education you've dreamed about. You have faced up to tough challenges before. You can survive all the late nights studying, taking tests, and writing papers. With good effort you can succeed in college. If I did it, I believe you can too!

—Mary Karr

Getting
In,
Getting
Started

Chapter 1

Going to College:
Lots of Help Is Available

Do you know that at many colleges the average age is about 30 and over half the students work while going to school?

Do you know that college instructors like students to form study teams to help each other pass courses?

Do you know that colleges and universities provide many free services to help you succeed?

A Dream Coming True

Going to college can be exciting and scary. The exciting part is that it is a dream come true. College is the pathway to knowledge, a new career, and a better future. Going to college is like venturing into a new world, a journey to a different life.

Like any adventure, however, it has its scary challenges....

Some Normal Fears and Concerns

Do you feel fearful about going to college? Concerned that your brain is rusty and that you won't be able to keep up with other students? Are you afraid that you can't afford college and yet don't see how you could work and go to college and raise your family? Feel guilty about depriving others while you do something that feels selfish?

If so, welcome to the club! *You are normal.* Most adult college students feel the same fears and concerns when they start. Yet they are succeeding in college and having the time of their lives!

How *The Adult Student's Guide* Will Help You

Every chapter in the book contains valuable information about how to succeed in college after you have been away from school for awhile. It will show you how to succeed even if you have a family, work, and have other important responsibilities.

The first section covers how to get started. **Chapter 2** shows how to *confront and eliminate many fears and concerns* reported by adult students.

Chapter 3 explains *how to make enrollment easy.* Most students need some form of financial assistance, so this chapter includes information on *how to finance your education.*

Part of being successful in new situations is to locate the resources available to you. **Chapter 4** provides information about how to locate the *many sources of help available* at your college.

The second section shows how to pass your courses with high grades. **Chapter 5** describes *how to succeed in college* and shows how to *increase your self-confidence.*

Chapter 6 provides practical information about how to manage your time and how to study using *the best, most widely used, effective study method.* Here you will learn how to reach a study goal, stop studying, and reward yourself. Self-motivated people have to learn how to be self-stoppers!

Nervous about taking tests? **Chapter 7** shows you *how to prepare for tests* so that you feel confident, less nervous, and score higher than you suspected you could.

Term papers are always a challenge. In **Chapter 8** you will find an excellent way to *write papers that get high grades.*

The third section provides guidelines for coping with serious non-academic challenges. **Chapter 9** shows how your *learning style* may create conflicts between you and your instructors and how to influence instructors.

Most adult college students have important relationships and commitments. In **Chapter 10** you will find many practical ways to gain *cooperation, support, and encouragement from others.*

Chapter 11 shows *how to combine working with taking college courses.* Most adult students work. A surprising number of employers offer special work schedules and reimbursement for courses completed. This chapter also has suggestions on what to do if you need a "bread and butter" job. **Chapter 12** discusses benefits of diversity on campus and in the workplace.

In many ways life itself is the real school. **The last section** shows how to make difficult situations turn out well. **Chapter 13** contains a simple but effective way to *handle pressure, reduce stress* and *develop healthy self-esteem.*

Could you succeed in a job that does not have a job description? **Chapter 14** shows *how to thrive* in non-stop change, gain strength from adversity, develop professionalism, and become skilled at learning lessons *in the school of life.*

Many adult students come to college searching for new or better careers. **Chapter 15** has valuable *career information* and many suggestions on ways to search for a new career.

At the end of each chapter you will find an **Action Review**. It is a checklist for reviewing how well you are putting into action what the chapter covered.

Dreams and Clocks

Clocks and dreams do not generally go well together but when you go to college you get up, eat, leave for school, arrive for class, study, and return home by the clock. You live by the clock from morning until night. Clocks help you reach your dream of a college education and a better life.

See clocks as helpers, not oppressors. Be creative! Use your imagination. You can learn effective time management skills. Visualize clocks such as this old-fashioned, three-legged alarm clock as leading you over stacks of books to your diploma. Remember, you need clocks when your dream for your future includes taking and passing college courses. Clocks are your friends.

Create a "Study Buddy" Group

As Barbara Sher says in *Teamworks!* "Everybody who ever succeeded and stayed human in the process had a lot of help...." and "People have more courage for each other than for themselves."

Many colleges now provide seminars or workshops for new students. If you can arrange to take one of these seminars your chances of succeeding in college will increase. Many adult students can't fit such classes into their schedules, however, so we want to encourage you to join with several other students in creating your personal support group. You'll be less lonely, develop good friendships, and help each other through tough moments. Guidelines for getting started are at the end of this chapter.

You are Special as a Student

Have you noticed that when you tell people about going to college they treat you differently? Mary Karr, who wrote the Foreword for us, started college shortly after her youngest daughter entered high school. Mary noticed an immediate change in how people treated her. She says:

> Before I started college, when my husband and I went to a party or social gathering, people would ask what I did. When I told them I was a housewife raising four children they'd say, "Oh," and start talking to someone else. On a scale from 1 to 100, I felt like I rated about a 3. After I enrolled, when people found out I was a college student, they'd say, "Oh!" I got treated like I had something important to say. My rating soared to the high nineties. The difference was fantastic!

One student reported that he needed to change his working hours by half an hour to make a night class. He hesitated about approaching his supervisor but finally spoke up. He asked for what he needed and explained why. From that day on his supervisor took a more personal interest in him and asked frequently about how school was going. Being a student can have some unexpected dividends!

The World Wants You to Succeed

Going to college is an exciting challenge. It will take hard work and some sacrifices but the benefits are worth the effort. The main point to understand is that *you are not alone.* There are many people and many resources available to you. The world wants you to succeed in your effort to better yourself!

How to Get a Support Group Started: Teaming Up With "Study Buddies"

Here are some guidelines for starting a College Success Group:

- Get together with a few other beginning students. Urge any new students that seem "lost" to come along.

- Meet in a place where you can sit comfortably and talk with each other, perhaps in the college cafeteria.

- Introduce yourselves. Keep repeating and checking that you have each others' names right as you talk and listen.

- Take turns talking about your feelings, impressions, and experiences starting college.

- Find out why you each decided to go to college. Ask about difficulties that have to be handled. Talk about your dreams and plans for the future.

- Ask about the courses you are each taking. Find out what program each person has selected or is considering.

- Make certain each person feels heard. By the time you finish, make certain each of you feels "A few of my classmates know about me and understand what I am feeling and experiencing right now."

- Discuss the benefits from having a small support group. Talk about why it will be useful to get together to study for tests, read each other's papers, problem solve difficulties, encourage each other, and applaud your successes.

- Plan to meet again soon to discuss what you are learning in this book about how to succeed in college. Read the chapters, for example, on ways to increase self-confidence and how to gain support from family and friends.

- Exchange telephone numbers and addresses. During the first weeks it will be useful to telephone each other often and meet frequently, and you may be able to share rides.

- Congratulate each other for having the courage to take this exciting, important step in life.

Chapter 2

Fears and Concerns: How to Confront and Overcome Them

Have you wondered if some of your fears about going to college are unrealistic?

Do you know that instructors enjoy teaching adult students and adult students often get high grades?

Do you know financial aid is available to older and part-time students?

Do you know that colleges, universities, and company training programs go out of their way to help adult students enroll and succeed?

So, I finally dragged myself over to the community college and took two courses. And, I was scared to death. I had been at war, in police riots, and a firefighter and that was all right. But, now I'm going to this college and I'm scared to death. I literally had stomach cramps—got physically sick. I really don't know why I was scared. I had no idea...no reason...it had nothing to do with anything...there was no consequence to pay...I could have gone over there, flunked out, and nothing would have happened. I would still have been a lieutenant in the fire department. Nothing would have changed. As it turned out, I left there with a 4.0 after taking four courses. But, when I first went through the door, I was dying.   —Bob DePrato

Facing Your Fears Takes Courage

In this book we will show you how thousands of people just like you found the courage to overcome their fears and succeed in college. We will show you how to develop the skills you need to increase your confidence. We will show you how to locate and use resources you never knew existed.

You may doubt your ability to succeed in college if you have not studied or taken tests for a long time, if you have to work, or have other responsibilities. It is possible, however, to be a successful college student and still handle other commitments.

You have overcome fears in the past by facing up to them and seeking information. You can do the same now. Before reading farther, take a minute to indicate how strong or weak your fear is about the following.

Strong—5   Moderately strong—4   Medium—3   Mild—2   Weak—1

1. __ I can't compete with younger students.
2. __ I won't be able to learn, my brain is rusty.
3. __ I can't do well in math.
4. __ I won't be able to study well.
5. __ Instructors dislike older students.
6. __ I won't fit in.
7. __ I won't have time for my family and other interests.
8. __ I can't afford college.

9. __ I can't work and study and raise a family.
10. __ Going part time will take me too long.
11. __ My family will feel neglected.

Common Fears and Concerns of Adult Students

If your total score from the above list is over 30 you definitely need to look through the following list of fears and concerns. They are typically felt and experienced by most adult students starting college. And like many fears you have experienced in your life, many of these fears are not realistic either.

I haven't studied in years. I'm out of practice. My brain feels rusty.
There is no evidence that older students can't learn and remember as well as younger students. This book will show you how to take notes, remember information from lectures and texts, and pass tests as well as any younger student.

I'm not sure I can read, write, or do math well enough to take college courses.
The college is happy to give you a free assessment of your skill levels to advise you what courses are best suited for you. If you need brush-up courses, they are available.

I was always nervous taking tests in high school. I'll be too upset to do well.
There is plenty of help available to show you how to reduce your anxieties about taking tests. College counseling and study skills centers provide help for students who need to learn techniques of test taking. Ask around.

I won't be able to compete. Only a few smart students receive high grades.
Times have changed! In the past many instructors graded "on the curve." They gave high marks to the few students who scored better than others in the class. Now, however, most instructors grade students on how much learning they accomplish during a course. Further, in many courses you will work on team projects with other students. This means

that you and other students work together to master the material and all get excellent grades.

> Don't be embarrassed if you can't do everything quickly.
> Don't try to compete with the young—compete with yourself.
> —*Eva Corazon Fernando-Lumba, age 78*
> *(Chosen by her college classmates to be the class speaker at commencement.)*

I don't have a high-school diploma, how can I take college classes?
Most community colleges will let you enroll for some courses *no questions asked!* You don't need a diploma. To qualify to enter a four-year college or degree program, you can take tests called *equivalency tests,* or GED, to earn a certificate that is the same as a high school diploma. Many community colleges also have a high school completion program called External Diploma Program, targeted for adults. This program considers work and life experience for credit. If you want to learn, there are many ways to do it without a diploma.

My past history in school is not good. I'm afraid they won't let me in.
Most community colleges and career training schools have an open-door policy. They care only about what you can do now. You may be happy to know that after accumulating 30 or more hours credit at a community college, most four-year colleges and universities will let you transfer in.

When my son sent applications to colleges, they all asked him for SAT or ACT scores. I know I couldn't do well enough on the college entrance exams to qualify.
The Scholastic Aptitude Test (SAT) and American College Test (ACT) are given to high-school seniors as a way to compare the seniors with each other in basic scholastic skills. Adult students do not usually have to submit these test scores. The academic assessment offered free by colleges takes the place of these nationally conducted tests.

I feel like a misfit, like an outsider in a strange world. I won't fit in.

The faculty, administrators, and students will be more friendly and helpful than you might imagine. Many younger students enjoy having older friends from whom they can learn and exchange views and experiences. Making friends like this can be some of the most enriching of your educational experiences. Besides, remind yourself that your tax dollars may have helped build the place. You have a right.

Instructors won't like having an older student in class.

You may be close in age to many instructors and have a lot in common with them. Most instructors enjoy and welcome adult students. These instructors welcome the life experience older students offer to a class. They often find communication is easier with you. Returning students are frequently more motivated to learn and pay closer attention to the instructor. Studies show older students tend to get better grades than younger students.

I was so nervous the first day of classes that I arrived at school 45 minutes ahead of the 9:00 class time. It was OK though, because I needed the time to keep running into the rest room—bladders seem so insistent sometimes. As I walked into the room for my first class I realized that my legs were shaking so hard I could barely walk. Fortunately, the front seat nearest the door was available so I quickly sat down. I tried to remain calm, but I knew I was trembling—my hands just wouldn't stop. After a *very* long time, the teacher came in and was ready to start the class. The first thing I noticed was how young she was and I thought to myself that school was going to be harder than I had imagined because how could this very young woman (she looked like a student herself) ever understand someone my age. Then I noticed that her legs were shaking! *She was nervous! Wonderful!* My day changed and was grand from then on. Oh yes,—I also found out that she was a graduate teaching assistant and that she was very sympathetic to all students. —MK

I can't afford college.

Most students qualify for some sort of financial aid. This may be in the form of scholarships, loans, grants, or employer reimbursements. And did you know that programs now exist where you can earn college credit for working? We will cover this in more detail in Chapter 3. College administrators and counselors are aware of the financial dilemmas facing returning students and will assist you in obtaining financial help. (See Resources and Suggested Readings on page 171).

I'm retired, I'd like to attend a few classes but I can't afford to pay tuition.

Many colleges allow older citizens to take classes at reduced fees, if space is available. You won't get credit for the course, but you can *audit* or attend classes at minimal cost. Look in the Sources section at the back of this book for where to write for information about 1500 colleges and universities that offer free or reduced tuition to older students.

I have young children, but I can't afford the cost of child care. How can I attend classes with children to raise?

Colleges are accommodating the needs of returning students. There are child care referral services at many colleges and women's resource centers. Many campuses offer low-cost child-care services for students. Colleges are doing much to assist people who have children. With young children it is very important to select healthful, reliable child care arrangements. Many student parents trade baby-sitting with other students, friends, family, or neighbors. Most colleges offer classes at night and on weekends. To work out a cooperative schedule one student takes day classes, the other night time or weekend classes. Some student parents vary days of the week with one taking classes on Monday, Wednesday, Friday, the other on Tuesdays and Thursdays. You can also inquire about courses available on video tapes at a learning center where you go through the material at your own speed, at a time that is convenient to you.

I don't think I can physically attend classes at the college campus.

There are some courses offered by modem on your computer or by the electronic classroom via satellite. Do you know that some college courses can be taken at home by watching broadcasts on television? Do you know that the college of your choice probably has correspondence or home study courses available? Inquire. You may be in for a pleasant surprise.

I cannot attend full time. It is hard to imagine all the years it will take to get a college degree.

A long journey starts with the first step. Once you become adjusted to being a student and gain confidence, you will probably be able to take more courses each term. In some cases, your life experiences and skills can be counted as credit toward your degree. In the next chapter you will see there are three ways to obtain college credit for what you already know, without taking courses. Or you might consider a shorter program. Many colleges offer two-year programs for people training for specific careers such as an associate degree in nursing. Regardless of the program you take, most students say their college careers go much faster than they thought possible.

My friends and family will suffer if I have to spend lots of time with schoolwork and my partner may feel threatened by my attempt to improve myself?

You will probably be surprised at how much your family and friends will support you in your new role as a student. Explain to them why you need to return to school. Show how your success will benefit all of you. Give them a chance and they will probably be very encouraging. Chapter 10 has a number of practical suggestions.

I have a heavy load at work. I have too many pressures to take college courses.

Did you know that many college courses are offered one evening a week? If you are willing to give up one evening a week you can take a college course. Employers are often willing to adjust workloads for employees in college, see Chapter 11. The time management tips in Chapter 6 will help. For guidelines on dealing with stress and pressure, read Chapter 13. The solution is to decide what you want in life and go for it.

If I become a student, I'll never have time for my family, friends, or outside interests. I can't take courses, study, and still have time for anything else.

It is true that you won't be able to do everything you did before and also be a college student. You will have to make some changes. But millions of people have gone to college while working and maintaining active personal lives. You are no different. If you follow the guidelines for succeeding in college, you'll do just fine and still have time for other important things.

I won't know anyone and I'm afraid to start out on my own.

Finding a "study buddy" will help you overcome those feelings quickly. It will not be long before you have supportive friends in each class, friendly fellow students who will help you feel you really belong and can succeed.

Anything is possible...

As you can see, there are ways to handle most of your concerns about being a college student. Many fears disappear when you confront them. As other fears or concerns develop, here are the steps to follow:

- First identify exactly what your fear or concern is. Write it down or describe it to someone. Then ask, "Is my worry based on rumors, or opinions, or is it a result of known facts?"

- To cope with problems or difficulties that might occur, ask other adult college students about their experiences. Find out if your fears are real.

- With specific, realistic problems, talk to an academic advisor or a college counselor. They will help you develop a realistic plan of action coping with the problem. Remember: *Don't be afraid to ask questions!*

Colleges and Company Training Programs Want You!

In the last few years higher education has changed. Colleges are spending a lot of money to attract and retain older students. Colleges arrange financial aid, employment, transportation (car pools and buses), housing, child care, personal counseling, medical coverage, and classes on how to study efficiently and pass courses. They provide counselors and advisors, recreational activities, and much more.

Did you know that the large, better companies are scrambling to find employees with basic skills? These companies will often pay trainees to take college courses, provide fringe benefits, and guarantee better jobs to graduates.

Now is a wonderful time to obtain a college education. Students of any age who want an education, advanced skills, or new careers can find support, resources, and encouragement.

Study Buddy Activity

Talk with each other about your fears and concerns. Then discuss how you can overcome or eliminate the fears and barriers. Keep in mind, too, that some problems can't be eliminated but it helps to talk about them with people who understand.

Chapter 3

Enrolling, Registering, and Financing Made Easier

Do you know how to enroll in college? What information to take with you?

Do you understand the difference between credit and noncredit courses?

Have you heard that you can turn some of your life experiences into college credit?

Do you know where to inquire about financial aid?

Do you know you can probably get financial aid if you need it?

Getting Enrolled and Registered

If you want to get a college degree from a four-year college or university, you must apply for admission and meet certain admission requirements before you can enroll. The friendly folks in the admissions office will explain what to do. Advisors and counselors help you get started.

Most community and technical colleges have an open door policy. That means they have few admissions requirements. No matter what your background, they will let you take a number of classes. It is possible to go to the campus or telephone, select the courses you want to take, fill out the registration forms, and pay tuition fees.

If you want to enroll in a specific vocational, technical, or degree program, however, we recommend that you speak to an advisor or counselor. It may be necessary to go through an assessment of your reading, writing, and math skills. If you need basic skill classes, the advisors and counselors will help you arrange to take them, often at little or no cost.

Community college and technical college classes can lead to a two-year associate degree, but the courses you take may or may not transfer to a university for a four-year degree. If you don't know what you want, check with the counseling or advising office. It is a free service and they will help you.

Credit, Noncredit, and Transfer Courses

The first thing to do is get a copy of the college catalog. Take your time looking through it. Learn how to tell the difference between a credit course, a non-credit course, and a transfer course. A *non-credit* course will not count toward a college degree. A *credit* course leads to a degree or certificate. You cannot earn a college degree by taking non-credit courses. A *transfer* course is a credit course that will be accepted by most four-year colleges if you wish your classes to lead to a four year degree.

You'll need to know what's ahead of you and what courses you will have to take. Your *catalog* describes all the courses available and tells you which ones you will be required to take if you want a degree or certificate. Read the fine print carefully.

IIII➡ NOTE: *The school catalog is a kind of contract.* The school agrees to award you a degree if you do all the required work as indicated in the catalog you used for your initial enrollment into degree course-work. Keep a copy for future reference.

If a course sounds interesting but is within a program for people majoring in that area, you might have to take a pre-requisite course before taking the one you wish. A *prerequisite* course is one that students must take and complete before they can get into a more advanced course. Some courses are so popular there are many classes during the day with many instructors. If you have a choice, find out which instructors students recommend and why they recommend them. Keep in mind that an easy teacher may not be the best for your learning.

Once you know the courses you want, look at a schedule of classes. The *schedule* will tell you the time, location, and instructor for each course. If you do not find what you want, call the department and ask the secretary when your course will be offered next and by whom. Department secretaries are a gold mine of information. Not every course is offered every term or semester.

Program Choices

You will need to decide how many courses and how many credit hours you want to try. A full-time student usually takes four or five courses totalling from 12 to 17 credit hours. The college may have a policy limiting the number of hours a student can take.

If you take two or three courses for less than about 12 credit hours, you will be considered a half-time or part-time student, depending on the college.

To help clarify the program choices facing you, here is a short summary of the vocational and academic programs available at most community colleges:

Associate Degrees—Require about two years taking a full load:
- General Studies—a combination of vocational courses, transfer courses, and basic skill building courses.
- Vocational—examples: nursing, diesel mechanics, dental assistant, computer science, television.
- Arts/Humanities—courses in writing, journalism, music, speech communications, theater arts (courses that transfer into four year degree programs at degree granting colleges or universities).
- Science—examples: biology, botany, chemistry, geology, math, computer science (transfer courses).
- Social Science—examples: psychology, sociology, political science, history, geography, economics, women's studies.

Transfer courses taken at a community college or enrollment at a four year college can lead to the following academic degrees:

Bachelor of Arts (B.A.)—Earned in a four year program emphasizing humanities and arts courses plus a foreign language at an accredited college or university.

Bachelor of Science (B.S.)—Earned in a four year program emphasizing science courses plus advanced level mathematics at an accredited college or university.

Master of Arts (M.A.) or Master of Science (M.S.)—Earned after the B.A. or B.S., taking approximately two years of courses in arts or science and writing a thesis.

Doctorates: Philosophy (Ph.D.), Education (Ed.D.)—Usually earned after the master's degree with advanced, graduate level seminar work and a doctoral thesis based on original research.

Registration Tips
If you have met with an advisor or counselor and know which courses you need, the college may allow you to register by mail or phone. This will save you much time.

If you must be present at registration, have all the forms filled out in advance and have a list of alternate courses. Plan to spend a lot of time standing in lines. Take your Social Security number with you because most schools use your Social Security number as your student identification number.

Be sure to have your checkbook or credit card with you. Most schools require payment at registration, although you may not have to pay the full amount then. Do not stay away because you don't have the full tuition at registration. Most schools have payment plans. Check with the office for financial aid if you have a financial concern. More about this later.

Don't Wait Until Classes Start

If you wait until the day classes start to enroll, you will find that many classes are already full. Once the allotted spaces are gone, no more students will be admitted. That is why it is practical to go to the college a few weeks or even a term ahead of registration to talk with an advisor.

If you want to enroll in a certificate program (usually one year) or in one of the degree programs (from two to four years) talk to an academic adviser at the college *a few months* before starting the program! Here's why:

1. You may need to take special examinations.
2. If you want to enter a degree program you will probably have to obtain a high achool transcript to show that you graduated and passed all required subjects. (Note: It takes time to obtain a transcript and it usually requires a small fee. You may run into delays if you don't send the fee with your request.)
3. You may have to take placement tests in English or math. Many entering students do not have the basic skills in math, spelling, grammar, and vocabulary. They need to brush up those skills in classes provided by the college.

Getting In After a Course is Full

If you must take a certain course at a certain time of day, but find that the course is already filled up, don't give up. There is a way to get in the class that can work. Even though you are not registered, attend the first class anyway. At the end of the class tell the instructor about your problem and ask for permission to enroll the course.

Most instructors, when approached in this manner, will allow a student into a course. The reason why showing up works so often, is because by the time the second week starts a few students who enrolled will have dropped the course. You need to be assertive to do this, but it is a way to get into a course you need.

Another option may be to go to another college in the area for the one course you need. Take the course and then transfer the credit back. Check with an advisor first to make sure the transfered credit will be accepted.

Prior Life Experience (PLE) Credits

Some colleges and universities offer prior life experience (PLE) credits or assessment for prior learning (APL). You may receive college credit for expertise you have acquired. For example, if you ran your own business for ten years and now wish to earn a business degree, PLE credit may be a possibility for you.

Educational institutions offering these credits usually have workshops to help you document your learning. A sizeable amount of writing and validation is required but you may be rich in life experience and able to qualify for official college credit.

Ronald, for example, served as a law enforcement officer for many years when he had to leave the force because of an injury. He had taken so many classes and workshops in law enforcement over the years that he received 56 credit hours as a result of a prior learning assessment. His case is unusual but demonstrates what is possible. Most students receive 10 to 20 hours credit for prior learning.

Jane had traveled extensively with her husband, a career military officer. She had visited most of the countries in Europe. She also could speak German fluently. With documented validation she was able to earn college credit in European history, sociology, and foreign language.

Marge wanted to complete a degree in home economics that she had started 25 years previously. She had managed a home, raised three children, and participated in many community service activities. When she read the course descriptions required for her major, she saw that her life experience fit nicely into some of the courses. She contacted an advisor and verified that PLE could be used toward her degree. She attended a class on documenting her experiences and was able to rapidly complete the requirements for a home economics degree.

Credits must be paid for, but when the push of time and experience is on your side it is an option to consider.

College Level Entrance Examination Program (CLEP)

For information about CLEP tests and how to arrange for them ask your college advisor. About 1500 colleges will accept CLEP scores for certain subjects. The subjects may have been studied in an advance course in high school or special training at work. The CLEP score subjects will be recorded on your transcript at your time of admission and count as credit toward graduation. You do not have to pay the college for the credits recorded.

Or You Can Challenge Courses

A third way to get college credit without taking courses is to challenge introductory level courses at the college. A more comprehensive description of the course work can be seen in a Course Content Guide often available through the department secretary. If you believe you already know a subject quite well, and the college allows, you can arrange to take the final examination in a course to see if you can pass it. If you do, you can get credit for the course by paying the normal registration fee. Keep in mind, however, that you may miss out on a valuable foundation for more advanced courses in the subject.

Buy Your Textbooks Early

After you have registered, go to the bookstore and purchase the required textbooks for your courses. The bookstore will have shelves full of textbooks for all the courses. Each shelf will list the instructor and course that the books are for.

Do not wait until after the first class meeting to buy your books because the bookstore may not have ordered enough books for everyone. They generally expect some students to drop the course and bring books back for a refund.

If you buy a used textbook pay close attention to which edition it is. Purchase only the most recent edition of a textbook. The instructor will not approve of your using a used second edition of a textbook when the third edition is now the one he or she uses.

When you purchase your textbooks keep your receipts and do not put your name in your books. If for any reason the course is cancelled or you do not want to stay in it, you can sell your books back to the bookstore for a full refund within a certain time limit.

Locate Your Classrooms

Once you know which courses you will be taking, go find the rooms where each of your classes will meet. Learn where each classroom is located and how you'll get from one room to the next. The day classes start, trying to find your way around campus can be more hectic than a shopping mall the last weekend before Christmas!

Courses Can Be Dropped

If, after attending the first or second class in a course you realize you've made a serious mistake, then consider dropping the class or transferring to another course. Remember, though, *it is normal to feel somewhat overwhelmed by a course at first*. Talk to the instructor or check with an advisor before dropping. If you drop a course early, most of your money may be refunded.

How to Get Financial Help

Financial assistance can be received through federal and state aid programs, scholarships, and loans. This assistance may help you pay the difference between what you can afford to pay and what it will cost you to go to college. Under federal and state aid programs all families and individuals are treated equally by a standardized evaluation of how much you and/or your family can afford to pay. Age is no barrier, but if you are under twenty-four, your parents income will be considered unless you are married or are a single parent.

Scholarships are frequently tailored to specific populations. Many funds are available for minorities and other special populations like displaced homemakers, women over a certain age, or students with special talents or career objectives. Examples include AARP's (American Association of Retired Persons) Women's Iniatiative 10th Anniversary Scholarship Program for women over fifty, Business & Professional Women's Foundation Scholarship, and the National Women's Relief Corporation. Unions and service clubs like Rotary, Elks, and Kiawanas are also worth investigating.

Loans can be through federal or state funds, private banks, or individuals. Do not forget to talk to family or friends who may feel it is the best investment in the world to help you get an education leading to a brighter future.

These People on Welfare Succeeded

Late one evening, 26 year old Carol sat with her baby in a bus station. Unmarried and on welfare, she had no money to pay for a room. Her life had been very rough. She felt that she was bad, abnormal, awful, and that life had passed her by. At that moment a well dressed woman sat down next to Carol and started talking with her. The woman was a college administrator. She said that she had once been on welfare.

The woman encouraged Carol to seek a college education. Carol had dropped out of school when she ran away from home at age 13. She knew she could not read, write, or do arithmetic very well. Carol went to a college and took some tests. They showed that she was learning disabled. With encouragement, however, she managed to learn basic skills and then pass the high school equivalency test. She obtained public assistance funds to take college courses. She found out how to obtain grants and student loans.

She got off welfare. She took as many courses as the college would allow each term. At age 30 she graduated with a B.A. with honors. Carol went on to earn an M.A. and now helps others find ways to finance their education. (See Sources, page 153.)

Gerald was laid off from an International Harvester plant when the farm recession hit in 1982. He applied for work at 380 companies with no success. He became homeless when his unemployment benefits ran out. He moved out of his apartment and lived for months in a rusty 1960 Mercury. When his car "died" he lived on the streets and did odd jobs whenever he could find them.

He heard about the Dislocated Workers Program, applied, and was enrolled in a community college. With financial aid, he became an A level student in accounting at the University of Iowa.

Fill Out the Forms

The office for financial aid has information about many sources of money for college students. Be prepared to fill out lots of forms. The forms can appear so overwhelming to the beginning student that some people walk away and never come back. Don't give up! *Many colleges give workshops in how to fill out the forms.* The financial aid personnel will lead you through the forms step-by-step, if necessary. There also is available at many college campuses a video tape that takes you through the application process.

Many colleges use the financial aid form (FAF) as a way to check eligibility for available scholarships. If you don't qualify this year, be sure to check again. The rules often change. Lack of eligibility one year is not necessarily true the next.

You can get ready to fill out the financial forms by preparing a rough budget of your expenses for the year. Your expenses will include: tuition and fees, books and supplies, room and board, transportation, and personal expenses.

Money is Available in Many Ways

Scholarships are only one form of aid or financial support offered to students. Many programs provide students with grants and loans. The computer can once more be a big help in accessing data for funds. A program called START contains a national database of over 300,000 scholarships, awards, loans, fellowships, and financial aid awards based on merit not financial need. A program called FUNDFINDER calculates the expected family contribution for college costs and locates approximately 3,000 private and state-sponsored programs. CIS (Career Information Systems) has a scholarship component and it is available in most employment offices. Your willingness to do your "homework" and fill out many application forms can make the difference in finding funds.

▶ NOTE: In the "Resources" section at the back of the book we have listed some internet addresses that are sources of current information about financial aid.

Funds With and Without Strings

A *grant* is an outright gift, which does not have to be repaid. In some instances, for a person who is without funds, the college may have a way to reduce tuition fees.

Many students qualify for loans at very low interest rates. Most student loans do not have to start to be repaid until after graduation. These funds are available from banks, from the federal government, and other sources.

Financial aid can be in the form of reduced tuition. A growing number of senior citizens are taking advantage of the free or reduced costs for people over 62 or 65.

If you are a veteran, you probably know about your GI benefits provided by the federal government, but do you also know that educational benefits may be provided by your state? The office of financial aid can tell you if you qualify.

The U.S. Department of Education makes funds available to college students through a number of programs:

Pell Grants at a community college can go up to $2300 for the first year for an undergraduate enrolled full-time; there can also be reduced funds available for students who can only enroll part-time. No payback is needed when your courses are successfully completed.

Supplemental Educational Opportunity Grants vary a great deal with the institution. One community college may provide $900 based on your need while a private college may have more funds available. No repayment is required on completion of course work.

Stafford Loans—vary according to need and institution. A community college may loan up to $2,625 the first year, $3,500 the second year. Other colleges with different tuition may increase or decrease this amount. There are subsidized and unsubsidized loans. *These loans do have to be paid back* if you stop attending college at least half-time for six months. A payment schedule is available; the entire loan does not come due at once.

Perkins Loans vary according to need and institution. Colleges can run out of funds so GET YOUR APPLICATION IN EARLY. Funds awarded can change from year to year.

New FAF forms come out in January for the following academic year. These may be mailed to you on request but often a personal appointment with a financial aid officer can give you current and exact information for your institution. Sometimes it can pay to shop different colleges and see where you can get the best financial aid package.

Don't Overlook Your Employer

Many employers reimburse employees for taking college classes. Sometimes the course work must be directly related to the job. Other times, they pay for all classes leading to a degree. Some unions have negotiated for significant academic benefits so their members can increase their job skills. In any case, it is worth checking with your benefit office or your employer directly. You may set a precedent for your company. If you are the first person at your work to receive tuition to increase your job skills you will be seen as an "up and comer", a person on the rise in your organization. Special arrangements might be made for you to take time off from work or to take your class right on your work site. Many companies bring classes right to the work site with TV classes. You will not know if you do not ask.

Jobs On and Off Campus

Another source of funds is through student employment programs. More information will be found in a following chapter. There are many jobs available for students who need income. The main point is that many possibilities exist for helping college students get an education. Don't rule yourself out without checking. Inquire to find out about your eligibility.

Action Review

☐ Have I read through the college catalog?

☐ Do I have specific courses in mind that I want to take?

☐ Have I found out if I need to apply for admission?

☐ Have I checked with the financial aid office to find out about my eligibility for financial assistance?

☐ Have I inquired about educational benefits or support from my employer?

☐ Do I know how to register for the courses I want?

☐ Do I know where my classrooms are located?

Study Buddy Activity

Talk about what difficulties you encountered trying to get registered for courses. Talk about the courses you plan to take. Help each other look into ways to tailor your selection of courses to fit your unique interests and needs. Be frank with each other about your financial needs. Someone in your group may know of a way to get extra financial help.

Chapter 4

Orientation: Getting Acquainted with Your Campus

Could you tell another student about all the free services available to you?

Do you know what recreation facilities are available?

Do you know where the health service is?

Have you found out about transportation services?

Do you know where to go with questions about class schedules?

Explore Your New Neighborhood

Remember what you do when you move into a new neighborhood? You explore. You don't passively sit and wait for someone from the "Welcome Wagon" to come knocking on your door with brochures about local businesses. Not at all. You go around visiting stores, businesses, and shopping centers in the area. You ask people for directions. You locate places that provide important services. You talk with neighbors to find out which places are best and which ones to avoid.

Starting college is like moving into a new neighborhood. The orientation leaders will give you stacks of information about college facilities and services available to you, but no matter how thorough they are, your own active exploring will be much more useful to you.

This chapter lists support services and facilities available at most colleges. Use it as a basic checklist of places to visit. If possible, visit every service or facility to get acquainted. Introduce yourself to staff members and ask what help they provide students. Don't be shy! All the college support services exist to help students like you succeed and graduate.

Make every effort to take guided orientation tours provided by the college. The tour leader will answer many questions that all of you have. Be sure to pick up a copy of the college newspaper. It is free, and the first edition of the new school year will be loaded with information for new students.

Remember: The more quickly you become familiar with the college campus, the more quickly you will feel comfortable in this new neighborhood.

College Services Checklist

Academic Advising

College counselors or academic advisors will give you information on course requirements for specific majors, eligibility for certain programs, and such. *Peer advisors*, specially designated adult students, may also be available to help you with your course selections and give you many useful tips.

➡ Find an advisor you enjoy talking with and meet with this person at least once a term. This can be one of your *most important* contacts.

Admissions Office—Orientation Office

On larger campuses these will probably be separate offices. On smaller campuses they may be combined. In any case, these are the offices with people who know the answers to your questions or know how to get the answers. That's their job!

Bookstore

Spend time browsing here to learn what they sell and where everything is located. The front part of the store usually contains *trade* books. These are books available to the general public and are sold in almost all college bookstores. The textbook section is at the back of the store. Textbooks will be arranged on shelves listed by course numbers within the different departments of the college.

Notice that computers, computer supplies, calculators, and other such items are priced at a student discount that is much lower than in regular stores.

Cashier/Business Office

Tuition and other money matters are handled here. Be sure to inquire about any available payment plans. The cashier's office will probably cash checks for any person with a valid student body ID card.

Center for Adult Students or Re-Entry Students

Many schools now have a designated area where older students, sometimes called *re-entry, adult learners,* or *non-traditional* students, can go for information about problems or concerns. It is also a place to meet a friend.

Cooperative Education

This is a specially designed program that lets you earn course credit as you learn new skills while working as a paid employee. It is a form of on-the-job training called "cooperative education." It is a college supervised program that lets you learn new career skills in a workplace setting. The employer gets certain tax breaks, you earn a modest wage and get course credit as well.

Counseling Center/Career Counseling
In these centers professional counselors are available for private sessions with students who want to talk about personal concerns. If you run into problems with instructors or other school personnel, counselors can serve as your advocate. Career counselors usually have access to an array of instruments/materials designed to help students clarify their career goals. These centers usually have books, cassette tapes, and other materials you can use or borrow. The services are usually free.

Child Care Center
If you have preschool children, the college may provide day care, or cooperative child care. You can bring children to school with you and for a low fee have the child cared for and fed by professionals while you are in school. Some colleges have provisions for school-age children to study on campus while parents attend night classes.

Dean of Students
The office of the Dean of Students is the place to go if you have questions or difficulties not handled well by other offices. The Dean of Students is responsible for seeing that you have every chance possible for succeeding in college. The Dean's office exists to help solve problems that may be interfering with your college success.

Dean of Instruction
This is an important office on every campus. Here you will find help with many kinds of academic questions and problems, including how to change a mistake in your transcript of grades, remove an incomplete in a course, get permission to take more than the allowed number of course hours, waive a course requirement, get into a course already filled, arrange for a special academic program, or complain if instruction for a course is not up to your expectations.

Office for Students with Disabilities

Special assistance will be available at little or no cost to help physically challenged or learning disabled students succeed. Such assistance may include notetakers, readers, writers, or sign language interpreters. The assistance counselors will have many practical suggestions. They can help students obtain adaptive equipment, transportation, and other services from your state's vocational rehabilitation department. Assessment for learning disabilities is available as well.

Health Service

Your campus has medical help available for emergency medical care and treatment. The health service may also be a resource for information, programs, and services on alcohol and drug abuse, birth control, blood pressure testing, cholesterol screening, and so forth. Costs are usually included in your fees or are very low. Inquire, if you wish, about student health insurance. Rates are low and the insurance may cover family members.

Learning Center

Many colleges have special centers where you go to learn a specific subject. You tell the person in charge what you want. You will then be assigned to a booth with a set of earphones, a television monitor, or a computer terminal. You work at your own speed at the lesson you are there to complete. You can stay with it as long as you wish. Don't feel intimidated; the person in charge will be glad to explain how everything works.

Library

Plan to take lots of time walking through the library on your own. Ask the librarians what would be useful for you to know. They usually enjoy telling students about all the library services. Take advantage of their helpfulness. Find out when they have sessions on how to use the library computers for locating books, references, and other information you will need for writing papers.

Notice that there are many desks, tables, and study areas. Most libraries have typing rooms, video viewing rooms, conference areas, and even quiet rooms for listening to music. For rest and relaxation (R&R), or research, this is one resource you should not overlook.

Registrar

The registrar's office keeps the academic records of all students. If you have earned college credit elsewhere, the registrar's office can give you information on how to claim credit and obtain documentation so that it will apply to your program. After you graduate, the registrar's office is the place that provides transcripts of the courses you took.

Security Office/Campus Police

The college has its own police officers. Find out how to call or reach campus security in case of an emergency. Call this office when any emergency help is needed. They may help with minor car problems or contact your family if you have an emergency. Make a special effort to be friendly with security officers.

Sports Facilities

All students have access to the sports facilities. There will be an exercise room, a swimming pool you can use for a relaxing swim, a track for jogging, and many other possibilities for exercise. You may be able to check out equipment free of charge.

> I found that during certain hours I could use the workout rooms used by the athletes! I could use the track and courts even if I wasn't taking a physical education class. And for a small fee I could occasionally take one of my daughters swimming. —MK

Student Activities Office

Every college has a number of student-run organizations. The student body president, other officers, and many student project coordinators are located in the student activities office.

Student Center

The student center is where you find cafeterias, art displays, television rooms, reading rooms, possibly a bowling alley, a barber shop, ping-pong tables, pool tables, lounging areas, and more. The student center on every campus is unique, so take time to familiarize yourself with this building. On the bulletin boards you will find announcements for various student activities such as theater productions and films shown on campus.

IIII➤ TIP: Find out if lockers are available for rent. A locker at school is a great place to leave heavy books, keep your lunch, or store an extra umbrella. It also serves as a place where friends can leave notes for you!

Student Employment/Job Placement Office
This office lists jobs that local employers have available for students looking for off-campus work. There are many jobs in every community that fit perfectly with being a student. This office will provide assistance with résumé writing and interviewing skills. They will help you find employment upon graduation.

Student Housing
Need a place to live? This office will help you. It will coordinate renting rooms in private homes and apartments in the nearby area. Your college may provide student housing in its own residence halls. Larger colleges will have housing for married students and their families.

Study Skills Center
Go here if you want help improving your study skills. This center has friendly, well-trained people who can teach you how to read faster, learn in less time, reduce your nervousness about taking tests, be better at passing tests, and write good papers.

Transportation Office
If you drive to school, go here to get a permit to park on campus. Check out this office before starting classes because parking space is often difficult to locate. Also inquire about car pools or buses as an alternative to driving your own car.

Explore Your College

Take time to get acquainted with your school in the same way that you would be curious about a new neighborhood you are moving into. Be active and curious, not passive or timid. Learn about the many resources and services available to you. You will feel comfortable about coming to campus more quickly, and the more you locate and use resources, the more successful you will be.

 REMEMBER: *The entire school exists to help you get the education you want!*

Action Review

☐ Have I explored the campus to find out what is available to students?

☐ Do I know where the health service is?

☐ Do I know how to reach campus security?

☐ Do I know where to inquire about transportation, day care, career counseling, and other services?

☐ Have I familiarized myself with the activities center?

☐ Do I feel well oriented to the college?

Study Buddy Activity

Plan a resources treasure hunt. Make up a list of places, offices, centers, and services you want to know about. Be sure to include the nearby neighborhood in your exploration. Find the location of stores, bank branches, the post office, copy centers, eating places, book stores, yogurt shops, and best pizza place. Split up into search teams. Divide up the list. Agree to meet at a certain place at a certain time. Afterwards talk with each other about what you found.

Guidelines
For
Succeeding
In
Your
Courses

Chapter 5

How to Succeed in College

Can you describe how ordinary people succeed as college students?

Do you know what it means to view college as a learning environment?

Do you know how to take good lecture notes?

Can you explain the affect of self-esteem on success in college?

I'm a single parent, low-income, first generation student and a black female. I'm surely one that sociologists would label as disadvantaged. But with the assistance of the special services program and my desire, my commitment and strong will to distance myself from the labels and statistics, I have achieved my goal of completing college.

—Edna Mae Pitman
1989 TRIO Achiever Award Winner
(One of 26 college students in the nation selected by the National Council of Educational Opportunity Association from more than 425,000 students in TRIO programs.)

Success in Each Course Leads to Success in College

You can do well in college without being an ideal student. Success comes from being motivated to succeed and doing the things that lead to success in your courses. Thousands of ordinary people who are nervous, have doubts, and who didn't stand out in high school do very well in college.

Research into student success shows that students who do consistently well in the courses they take are those who:

- find out at the first class meeting when all the tests will be held and when papers or projects are due.
- attend all classes.
- prepare for each class in advance.
- ask several good questions during class.
- take good lecture notes.
- organize their time well.
- study regularly.
- set specific study goals each time they study.
- hand in course work on time.
- prepare for tests by writing practice tests.
- stop studying when they reach their study goals.
- work well with other students on group projects.

In addition, successful students are self-motivated, appreciate and encourage other students, have strong self-esteem and self-confidence, develop good study habits, and associate with other successful students. More about this later.

Find Out What is Required

Successful students actively determine the requirements for each course. During the first lecture they get answers to these key questions:
- Which chapters in the textbook will be covered?
- When will the exams be given?
- What material will each exam cover?
- What type of questions will be on the exams—essay, multiple choice?
- Are there past exams on file in the library?
- Will other work be required?
- When will the work be due?
- How will grades in the course be determined?
- What are the instructor's office hours? The location?
- Does the instructor have an outline of the most important terms and concepts to be covered?

These questions are a starting point. Others will occur as you go along. This is why having the phone number of another student in each of your classes can be very useful.

Many instructors provide a handout called a course syllabus. If you don't receive a handout, be sure to write everything down in your notebook. After class compare notes with other students.

Get Ready for the Avalanche:
The Smartest Way to Organize Your Notebooks

We suggest that you purchase a separate, three ring notebook for each course. Select a different color notebook for each one. This helps avoid the "Oh no! I can't believe I brought the wrong notebook today!" experience. Be sure to write your name, address, and phone number in each notebook.

Purchase notebooks that have at least five color tabbed sections: the first contains the course syllabus and any other instructions specific to the course; the second holds paper for your class notes; the third holds assignments ready to hand in;

the fourth holds assignments/tests handed back; the fifth includes extra handouts from your instructor.

How do you place all the handouts into a three ring notebook? Either purchase a small, inexpensive hole puncher or find the location of a three hole puncher you can use.

Organizing your course materials in this way will make it much easier to be a successful student. Reminder: *After going to all this trouble, be sure to take your notebook and a pen to each class!*

Take Good Lecture Notes

Getting a good grade in a course starts with taking good lecture notes. The nature of human memory is such that people soon forget most of what they hear no matter how much they intend to remember.

Several days after a lecture, most students can recall only a small percentage of what the instructor said. If you ask a student who doesn't take notes to tell you about some details about what the instructor said last week, you will quickly see how important note taking is for accurate recall. So, unless you tape record the lectures or trade note taking with a classmate, you need to take notes at every lecture.

Always take notes in the same notebook. Date each day's notes. Always follow the last lecture with notes from the next lecture. Do not mix lecture notes from different courses and different days in the same notebook.

Lectures are like textbook chapters. Each usually has a main theme and makes several important points supported by examples and/or facts. If you listen for them, they will be easier to hear.

It is best to take lecture notes in an outline form. This technique will help you identify the main points that are likely be show up as questions on exams. The outline form for lecture notes looks like this:

The major topic or subject.
A. Major division or category within the topic.
    List important statements.

1. history, facts, experiments, first researcher.
2. second researcher, other experiments.
    a. supporting facts and details
    b.
    c.
  3.
B. Second major division in the topic area.
    1. facts, new perspectives, research.
    2.

Guidelines for Taking Notes
1. During the lecture, take notes on the right-hand side of the paper. Leave a wide margin on the left.
2. Write down complete phrases and statements, rather than single words.
3. Star, highlight, or underline points the instructor emphasizes.
4. As soon as possible after the lecture, complete unfinished sentences and fill in material you didn't have time to write. The next time you study you will turn your outline into test questions. Each lecture will usually supply you with five to seven good exam questions. Write them in the left-hand margin.
5. Leave the back of each page blank. Use it later for taking study notes and writing questions from other sources such as your textbook or assigned reading.

This procedure will help you organize lectures into questions and answers. Plan to come out of each lecture with several questions and answers. They are likely to be on the next test!

Sample Notes
If your notes are neat and as close to outlined as possible, you'll have a much better chance of turning them into a good set of questions. These notes were taken at an introductory psychology lecture. The topic was learning.

Intro Psych - November 17
LEARNING
    A. Behavior Modification - First researcher B.F. Skinner
        1. Main principles:
            a. Experimenter must wait for a behavior to occur.
            b. Behaviors reinforced tend to increase
               (Note: Term is *reinforcement*, not *reward*)
            c. Behaviors ignored tend to decrease
            d. Behaviors punished may be temporarily
               suppressed but may increase, punish-
               ment can be reinforcing!
        2. Tracking positives plan:
            a. Specify the desired observable behavior.
            b. Choose an effective reinforcer .
            c. Measure current level of desired behavior.
            d. Watch for slightest increase in the desired
               behavior.
            e. Give reinforcer as fast as possible.

    B. Classical Conditioning—First researcher Ivan Pavlov
        He noticed dogs salivating when a bell
        rang that signaled feeding time.
        1. Focus on automatic reflexes.

From notes such as these it is easy to develop practice questions that come close to what the instructor will ask. Note: Using your own abbreviations for frequently repeated words can be helpful. Just make sure you can understand your own abbreviations!

Are You An Active Learner?

It is important to learn how to take good notes because in college the responsibility for learning is the student's, not the teacher's. You cannot sit back passively and expect instructors to entertain you. It is not an instructor's responsibility to push you to learn or to make sure you get your assignments done, not like it may have been in high school. Succeeding in college is your responsibility, and that means being an active learner.

Are Your Goals Self-Chosen?

Success is to reach a goal. Successful students are students who choose and reach their goals. Getting to any goal you select and work for makes you successful.

The key is to make certain your goals are self-chosen. It is less motivating and less satisfying to have goals that others have selected for you.

If you do not have specific career goals or personal life goals, read Chapter 15 now. Talk with counselors in the careers center at your college. There is a wealth of helpful information available.

I got top grades. Mostly, it was because I attended all classes, and generally put a lot of time and effort into learning. However, I also made sure that every teacher knew my name by the end of the quarter. I always sat in the front of the room, and asked one or two intelligent questions during every class (the sort of question developed only by studying the class material outside of class). Once I felt that the professor recognized me as a student that cared about the material covered in the class, I made an appointment during office hours and pursued some other aspect of the course material with the professor. In this way, I was able to get the person to add a name to the face of the inquisitive and interested older student who sat in the front row. I'm sure that where my grade was borderline a couple of times, I was given the advantage because of the reputation I so carefully cultivated for myself. It couldn't have hurt.—MK

Good Study Habits Are Very Important

Your habits determine how much you learn during the time you spend studying. Two students may spend the same amount of time in classes and studying, but the student with good study habits learns more and gets a better education than the student with poor study habits. The chapters ahead will describe good study habits and show how you can develop them.

Enjoy Reading and Learning

Marion Drake, an instructor who works with adult students, says to buy a good dictionary and enjoy learning about the meanings of words. "We do best what we do most," she says, "so stop watching television. Spend lots of time reading." She says develop a passion for the subject and don't just memorize terms, learn what the concepts and principles mean.

Action Review: Checklist for Success

☐ Do I act in ways that lead to success in my courses?

☐ Do I have well organized course notebooks?

☐ Do I take good lecture notes?

☐ Am I an active learner?

Study Buddy Activity

Make up a your own lists describing successful and unsuccessful students. One of you write the lists down on a sheet of paper. On one list describe what a student can do to increase chances of succeeding. Then to provide contrast, make up a second list of what students do that reduces their chance of succeeding. Include what attitudes and habits you believe help or hinder success in college.

To have extra fun with this activity, each of you arrange to interview several students that you see as successful. Find out what they say about why they are successful. Get back together and compare what you learn from them.

Note: If you write out a summary of your two lists for each other to have, please mail us a copy. The address is at the end of the book. Some students get very creative. The poem on the next page is what one student shared with us. (It is reprinted here with her permission.)

A Is For **Attitude**
The Alphabet of Success

A is for **Attitude**, it's where it all begins.
B is for **Believing** in yourself to the end.
C is for **Caring** enough to do your best.
D is **Doing** more than just passing the test.
E is for **Enjoying** the life that you live.
F is the **Future** rewards school will give.
G is for the **Goals** you plan to achieve.
H is for **Hanging-In-There** when tempted to leave.
I is for **Imagining** the things you can do.
J is for **Judging** the false from the true.
K is for **Knowledge** and nothing beats this.
L knows that **Labor** can be an abyss.
M is for **Mistakes** which we all make sometimes.
N is **Not Letting** them keep you behind.
O is the **Omnipotent** power we possess.
P is for **Plowing** the fields of success.
Q never **Quits** because that's defeat.
R stands for **Respect**, a two-sided treat.
S is for **Support** that we need to help us through.
T is for **Time Management** and for **Trying**, too.
U is **Understanding** how things should be done.
V knows the **Value** of having some fun.
W is the **Wisdom** to be the best you can.
X is a **variable**, like in algebra, man.
Y is **Your** choice to be something more.
Z is the **Zenith** we are all reaching for.

—Lynn Reese

The Best Way to Study

Do you know how to create study schedules?

Do you know how to set study goals?

Do you work on high-priority items while ignoring less important matters?

Have you learned the most widely used and effective way to study?

Do you know that your studying time can be reduced by reading to answer questions?

Have you arranged a good study area for yourself?

Do you use principles of psychology on yourself when you study?

Start By Listing Study Goals

Study goals help you focus your time and energy. They help you take the step-by-step actions that lead to reaching your dream for a better future. Setting goals is one of the best ways to motivate yourself to study efficiently and effectively.

Students who don't set goals or schedule their time are usually uncertain about what to do from hour to hour. Students who identify what they should study to pass a course and create a schedule to achieve their study goals, usually succeed more easily than they imagined. Here's how to set study goals and design a schedule to achieve them.

Determine What Your Study Goals Should Be

First, you have to ask, "What do I have to do to pass the course?" In most courses you have to do the following:

- Attend class.
- Participate in class discussions.
- Pass quizzes.
- Write papers.
- Pass tests.
- Complete projects.

To set up a study schedule ask these questions:
1. When is each test, paper, or project due?
2. How can I space my studying so that I don't put everything off until the end?
3. How much should I do each day if I wish to accomplish everything on schedule?

Answering these questions will allow you to design an effective schedule for reaching your study goals. You will know what to do and know when you can stop!

How to Manage Your Time

Fill in Your Calendar

Your greatest aid will be a calendar with spaces that you can fill in with important dates and obligations. Obtain a big year-at-a-glance calendar or a monthly calendar that you can tear apart and pin up on your wall. You want to be able to see at a glance what is ahead for the entire term or semester.

Fill in dates when examinations are scheduled and when papers and projects are due. Fill in all the times that you plan to do things with your family, meetings, concerts, and other events.

Create Weekly Schedules

Once you have a picture of your major commitments for weeks and months ahead, you can make up a weekly schedule of your classes, study hours, and other obligations. A weekly schedule organizes what you do with your time. It shows you the places where you have extra hours you can use for studying. A schedule decreases the amount of time you waste.

When making your schedule:
- Budget some time to prepare for each class by reviewing notes and creating questions.
- Designate time for personal responsibilities.
- Reserve time to study course notes and write questions as soon as possible after each class.
- Study difficult subjects when you will have the least interruptions.
- Schedule time with your family and other important activities.

When you create good time management/study schedule, it will motivate you. In fact, some students get so carried away we need to caution you to discipline yourself to stop studying! When you reach the scheduled time to stop, go get some exercise or do whatever you want to do. *Practice being a self-stopper!*

The problem for some students is that they study so much they use their time inefficiently. C. Northcoat Parkinson observed that "work expands to fill available time." You may have experienced this phenomenon. Let's say that you had in mind cleaning up the house during three hours available on Saturday morning. If you have three hours available, it will probably take you three hours to get the job done.

But let's say that before you start to work you learn that a very special person is coming by to visit and will arrive in about 30 minutes. You would probably be able to clean the house reasonably well in fewer than 30 minutes. What we suggest is that you decide what has to be done, do it, and then stop.

Time management experts often say that things not worth doing are not worth doing well. With less important jobs or matters don't waste precious time doing them as well as you can. Do them quickly, just good enough to get by. Use your precious time for more important things.

The main thing to accomplish is to control your activities rather than letting your activities control you!

A weekly time schedule that lets you fill in every half hour of the day, from early morning until late at night, will show you that you have many more hours each week than you might have ever realized. (Note: It will help your family if you post a copy where they can see it.)

Make Daily "To Do" Lists

Take a few minutes each evening to list the important things that you have to do the next day. List those things most important to be done, then plan ahead. Here's what one student reported doing:

> On a daily scale, I prepare myself by getting my book bag ready to go out the door the night before. I make sure I have paper, pens, books, calculator—everything I will need for the next day's classes. This saves much searching time and also reduces stress the next morning. Along with all the supplies I *will* need, I make sure there is nothing in my bag that I *won't* need. This includes extra books, note pads, tennis shoes, a broken door handle—anything just along for the ride.

Your "to do" list gives you a way to make decisions about what you do during the day. It reminds you what is important to do and what to say "no" to. It also lets you know when you are done.

Get in the habit of putting your time and energy into your highest priority items. Don't deceive yourself by thinking that you will get to the really big project after you get all the little things out of the way. What happens is that by the time you finish the little, unimportant tasks your time is gone and you are too tired to work on the important project. The same student quoted above says:

> To me the most important thing is *putting first things first*. A set study time is a priority. Once time is decided upon, decide what needs to be done and *do it*. One way I can remind myself of the importance of my commitments is to picture the result of my actions. I ask myself "How will watching TV instead of studying affect my future?" This puts things in perspective and reminds me of my priorities.

Your Study Area

The environment where you study affects how well you learn. Here are some tips about what to do and not do:

Study in the same place at home and at school. Don't keep changing your studying locations. New places distract you.

Create a study area for yourself at home. Do what you can to make it the place where your attention is devoted entirely to your studying. If you study at a desk, keep it cleared off.

Use a comfortable chair. It will be a good investment to get a comfortable chair that adjusts for height and back support. Discomfort can lead to muscle strain and physical distractions.

Arrange good lighting. To reduce eye strain, your room should be well lit, with the main light source off to one side. A light directly behind or in front of you will be reflected from the glossy pages of your textbooks. A constant glare tires your eyes more quickly than indirect lighting. If you can't shift the lamp, shift your desk. Place the desk so that no portion of the bulb shines directly into your eyes.

If you wear glasses, consider having them tinted slightly. Older eyes are vulnerable to eye strain.

I loved my study area. My kids kept giving me posters to hang on the wall, and soon I felt that my corner was like the typical student's study area. Over my desk was my favorite Tom Sellek *Magnum PI* poster with Tom standing on the beach wearing shorts. Tom and I spent a lot of hours together, and I can still visualize that poster.—MK

Neutralize Noisy Distractions

Use steady background sounds to neutralize distracting noises. Play your radio or stereo system *softly* while you study to create a steady background of "white noise" to mask occasional sounds. Experiment with stations, tapes or CDs until you find what works best for you. Instrumental (non-vocal) music is usually best.

▶ Don't try to study with the television on.

If you want to watch a TV program, then watch it. But don't try to avoid feeling guilty about watching television by having your book open to read during commercials. Studying with the TV set on is *academic suicide*. Use television time as a reward after you have completed a study period, if you wish.

The Big Picture

Every person who is both busy and effective makes decisions about what to do and what not to do with their time...

You started with your dream.
You decided that going to college was the way to reach your dream of a better life.
You confront your fears and concerns.
You select courses that lead to what you want out of college.
You imagine yourself succeeding in your courses.
You identify what you have to do to pass each course.
You develop monthly and weekly schedules for doing what it takes to complete course requirements.

You make "to do" lists that help you focus on your highest
   priority activities each day.
You stick with your daily schedule.
You balance being a self-starter with being a self-stopper.
You make a plan that leaves time for your
   family, your job, and other important activities.
You become very good at learning, passing tests, and get-
ting high grades.

What Psychologists Know About Learning

Psychologists have studied how people learn for almost 100
years. You can use their research findings to improve your
ability to learn and remember. Their research also helps show
what interferes with learning and remembering.

Here are some important principles to understand:

- The weakest form of learning is *passive recognition*. Studying is not the same as reading your Sunday newspaper.
  Reading your textbook is not the same as reading a novel.

- The strongest form of learning is *active recall*. This learning
  method is to read the material with curiosity, intending to
  remember what you read, and then from memory write or
  verbally give a summary of what you learned. Passively
  reading your textbooks and lecture notes over and over
  again is no fun and is an inefficient way to learn.

- How well you first learn and then later recall what you
  study is influenced by your study environment, study plan,
  and learning style.

   The purpose of any test is to measure what you have
learned. This means that to pass tests you must start by learning
the information you will be tested on!
   Textbooks are not written to entertain you. When it comes
to studying, you must use study techniques that motivate you
to mentally reach out and grasp important information.

Have You Had Trouble Learning?

Your past experience in school may not have been the most positive. Perhaps you couldn't spell your way out of a paper bag and this turned you off from writing assignments. Maybe you reverse numbers and still have trouble with phone numbers and your checkbook. You can understand if you are told instructions, but not if you read them—or vice versa. You may have had a learning disability and never known it.

Sometimes the trouble you have with learning can be inherited. If your father or mother or grandparent had great difficulty spelling, you may have great difficulty spelling. Other times, difficulty in learning can be caused by an injury or illness. The Office of Disability or Counseling Office can help evaluate your difficulty and assist with tools to compensate. The American Disability Act 504 mandates schools provide the assistance you need to develop your potential. Figures for school children diagnosed with learning disabilities show a more than 250% increase since 1975. When you last went to school, learning disabilities may not have received adequate attention.

Tips received from those who have special needs are included in the acronym LEARNING:

L Let instructors know how they can help you.
E Expedite Extra time on written or oral tests.
A Art work and color coding 3x5 cards helps memory.
R Record lectures on cassette tape.
N Need to keep Noise and visual distractions to a minimum.
I Include tutorial help for difficult subjects.
N Notify adminstrators about problems you encounter.
G Get a computer with a spelling and Grammar checker.

Everyone has strengths and weaknesses in learning. The trick is to accentuate your strengths and shore up your weaknesses.

Remember, learning disability has nothing to do with intelligence. Einstein, Leonardo Da Vinci, Thomas Edison, Cher, and Tom Cruise are all known to have learning disabilities.

The Secret to Rapid Learning and Success in Classes: Ask and Answer Questions

The most effective learning technique is very simple. It is develop the habit of reading textbooks, taking lecture notes and studying by asking and answering questions. When you do this you save many hours studying and have time to spend with your family, hold a job, take trips, attend concerts, and lead a balanced life.

Learning this study technique will take some effort because you will probably have to change some old reading habits. Such changes can be difficult. In the long run, however, the benefit is worth the effort, so stick with it.

How to Increase Your Studying Efficiency, Comprehension, and Ability to Remember

If you want to spend less time studying and remember better, focus on figuring out the important questions and the answers to them. The following steps will increase your learning speed, comprehension, and memory. Here is how to do it:

Skim Through Each Chapter Looking for Sources of Questions

You are sitting at your desk. The instructor has told you what chapters to study in the textbook. You open the textbook. Do you start reading the textbook as though it is a novel? No! Here is what to do:

First, look at the beginning of the chapter to see whether or not there are chapter objectives or a list of questions. Read them.

Second, look at the end of the chapter to see if there is a chapter summary. If so, read it right away! This is where you will find the important points the authors wish to stress.

> When reading textbooks you decrease your study time by reading the chapter objectives and the summary at the end of the chapter before reading the chapter! (Quick test: Did you do that with this chapter?)

Third, skim through the chapter quickly. How do you skim a chapter? Glance through it rapidly the way you would look at a magazine that you are considering buying. You want a picture of the forest before you examine any trees. Look for titles, subtitles, illustrations, pictures, charts, highlighted words or phrases, and statements that will give you a basic idea of what the chapter is about.

Fourth, skim the chapter a second time turning titles, subtitles, and highlighted terms into questions. For instance, "Maslow's Hierarchy of Needs" is a section heading in a psychology textbook. When you see such a heading ask yourself "What is the hierarchy of needs that Maslow described?"

By asking questions about the material in the chapter, you alert yourself to the important points in the chapter. Reading in this manner is active rather than passive. When you ask questions, you will quickly develop a good sense of the questions the instructor will ask on tests.

What does a good question look like? It usually starts with a phrase like:

> Name three kinds of…
> _____ is an example of what?
> Describe the ways that…
> List the important points about…
> The pioneering research was done by…
> The early research proved…
> What does _____ mean?
> The definition of _____ is…
> The three stages of development are…

Read to Answer Questions
Now it is time to read. Read fairly rapidly. Read to find the answers to questions you asked while skimming the chapter.

IIII➡ In many instances, your questions and answers will be in titles, subtitles, or lead sentences and chapter summaries.

As you read, if you come to the answer to material that raises a new question, slow down, ask and then answer the new question.

Write a Summary

After you read the chapter to answer your questions, close the book. Write a short summary of what you have just read. You learn best when you write a summary of the main points and facts from memory.

Recite What You Remember

If you commute in your own car or have a place where people will not be bothered by your talking out loud, a second way to learn course material rapidly is to verbalize what you have just read. Plan to take a few minutes skimming through the textbook before starting your commute. Then as you drive along, talk to yourself out loud about what you just learned.

The more sensory systems and muscles you involve in your learning the faster and more long lasting your learning will be. Talking to yourself shows you are study-smart!

Students who are not study-smart waste a lot of time by reading textbook chapters over and over without proving to themselves that they truly learned the contents of the chapter. They think, "I read it, I underlined it, I know what it's about." *Don't make that mistake!* Prove to yourself that you comprehend the chapter by answering questions out loud and writing chapter summaries.

IIII➤ Underlining or using a yellow highlighter will not lead to remembering nearly as well as writing or reciting what you know!

Make a List of Terms and Concepts

The fastest way to master a new subject is to focus on learning what the terms and concepts mean. To accomplish this quickly, make a list of words, terms, principles, and concepts that you will be expected to define, explain, describe, or understand.

Many students find that 3 x 5 cards are useful. You write the term, concept, or principle on one side of the card. On the reverse side you write out the definition or explanation. Then, when it is time to recite and review what you know, you look at the card and try to state or write from memory the definition written out on the other side.

Using 3 x 5 cards is handy because you can carry them around with you instead of your textbook. When you have a few minutes after lunch, on the bus, or while waiting for a class to start you can use the time to review your definitions.

⯈ You do not need long blocks of time to study. You can study for a few minutes any time, any place!

Some commuting students make cassette tapes listing important terms and concepts. They use the tapes to give themselves an oral quiz as they drive along.

Review Frequently

Frequent reviews help anchor your learning. With written summaries and 3 x 5 cards you can go over what you've learned at any time. And, as you will see in the next chapter, you are well prepared to write practice questions.

The Benefits

This study method is simple, saves time, and it works! You study for a limited time and then stop with a feeling of confidence that you know the material. You spend less time rereading chapters and doing other time-consuming study activities. This study method gives you the feeling that you've mastered the material. When you know you can answer questions correctly and make accurate summaries, you feel confident. Here is what one student wrote on an evaluation at the end of a course:

> When I read this chapter I thought "Oh, come on! It can't be that simple." But yes, Virginia, it is that simple. What a difference it has made! I was taking an economics course and getting nowhere...I started studying this way and was amazed at how much I retained. I've also found that the method of writing questions during lectures works well. It gives me a good idea of what is likely to show up on tests.

Some Difficulties With Skimming, Asking Questions, and Summarizing

Changing old reading habits is not easy. Especially if you are used to reading every word, and are trying not to miss something. You have to use your mind actively when you ask questions and write summaries. This takes more energy than passively reading printed pages. On the other hand, you learn so fast with this method you may feel that something is wrong because you are not having to study as much as you thought it would take to get good grades!

Train the Way Athletes Do

This method is similar to the way athletes prepare for competition. Imagine yourself agreeing to run in a ten kilometer race several months from now. You will run with friends and it is important for all of you to do well. To be at your best, would you loaf around until the last few days and then prepare by running day and night until the time of the race? No. You'd start now with a weekly schedule of jogging and running. A little bit of practice on a regular basis prepares you the best. The same approach is true for effective studying and remembering.

When you use these study techniques you can expect the following results:

- The quality of your questions and answers will improve with practice.
- The amount of time it takes you to ask questions and write good summaries will decrease.
- You will be able to cover large amounts of material in far less time.
- You will find that you think up the same questions that your instructors ask.
- Your study periods will be shorter and you will feel comfortable stopping when your study goals have been reached.

Work With Your Concentration Span

Have you ever sat reading for awhile and then suddenly realized you didn't know what you just read? Discovered that your mind wasn't paying attention to what your eyes were reading? This is not an uncommon experience for students.

The problem is that while you can make yourself sit and read hour after hour, your mind will take a break when it needs one. You are human. The length of time you can make your mind concentrate on a subject is limited even if you can make your body sit at a desk for hours.

Are you a morning person? Set the alarm for 5 a.m. and study before the rest of the household is up and leave chores for evening when your brain is disengaging. Does nap time after work help you feel mentally alert and full of "get up and go?" Or, can you get more done late into the night? If so, then go ahead and study until one or two in the morning. Select the time of day to study when your mental juices are most alert.

The way to make your study time more productive is to start with what you can do now and build on that. On the average, how long can you study before your mind slips off to something else? Twenty-five minutes? Ten minutes? Most students can concentrate on a textbook 10 to 15 minutes before starting to daydream.

Record Your Study Time Segments

The next time you study, write down the time you start. Record how long you read textbook material before your mind starts to daydream. Don't set any particular goals for yourself yet. First, you have to find out the typical amount of time you spend reading textbook materials before your mind starts wandering.

Let's say that you find your average concentration span is about twelve minutes. This is the typical length for most beginning students. It does not mean that you have an Atttention Deficit Disorder. Accept ten to twelve minures as your current level. Don't be bothered or upset thinking that you can't control your mind. Focus instead on increasing your concentration span in small, reasonable amounts.

Take Mandatory Breaks

Set up a study schedule that fits your concentration span. Take a short stretch after each study segment and a long break about once an hour.

You will probably find the end of a study segment coming so quickly you will want to continue. *Don't continue without your break!* Keep your agreement with yourself. If you decide to take a stretch break after each short segment, then do so. *Do not allow yourself to study more than the allotted time.* Get up and stretch. Get a drink of water or step outside for a breath of fresh air or a hug from a loved one before starting the next study segment.

Mix Study Subjects

Here are more principles of learning:

- When you learn one set of facts and then follow it with similar facts or material, the second set will interfere with your memory of the first and the first will interfere with your memory of the second.

- When you try to learn lots of information at one time you remember the first items and the last items best. The middle is most difficult to recall.

When Steve came into the learning center he was tired and discouraged. He worked full time, was enrolled in three night courses, and studied many hours evenings and weekends. As hard as he studied, however, he found it difficult to remember the material the way he felt he should.

Did Steve have a memory problem? No. His problem was that he would study one subject all evening or all morning and then switch to another subject the next day.

The more you try to learn similar material at one time, the worse your recall will be. How can you avoid this problem when you have lots of material to study? The best way is to mix your study hours with dissimilar material.

▐▐▐▶ Do not devote one long study period to one subject.

Switch subjects about once an hour. Always try to make your new subject as different as possible from the subject you have just finished. That way your mind can be assimilating one topic while you are reading about another.

Principles of Learning in Action

Here is an example of a study schedule using the principles described above:

15 min.—history
   1 min. stretch break
15 min.—history
   1 min. stretch break
15 min.—history
   10 min. break—drink
   some water, walk the dog
15 min.—math
   1 min. stretch break
15 min.—math
   1 min. stretch break

15 min.—math
   10 min. break—drink fruit
   juice, make short
   phone call
15 min.—English
   1 min. stretch break
15 min.—English
   1 min. stretch break
15 min.—English
All done! Reward—watch
video tape of *Home Improvement*.

Now that you know how to use the principles of learning to study efficiently and effectively, the next chapter will cover how to prepare for tests.

Action Review: Checklist for an Effective Study Plan

Use the following to rate how well you are doing at studying and following an effective learning plan:

❏ Do I have a calendar for the term marked with dates of all tests and assignments?

❏ Do I make weekly schedules of my classes and activities?

❏ Do I use daily "to do" lists?

❑ Can I do less important things quickly? Just good enough to get by?

❑ Do I set specific study goals for each course?

❑ Do I set up a schedule to achieve study goals?

❑ Do I skim chapters first, ask questions, read the summaries, and then read to answer questions?

❑ Do I practice writing answers to questions and write chapter summaries?

❑ Do I make up lists of terms and concepts to use when I test my ability to recite definitions from memory?

❑ Have I created a good study area for myself?

❑ Do I study in short time periods and take breaks?

❑ Do I switch study subjects often?

❑ Do I stop studying when I said I would?

❑ Do I reward myself when I have successfully accomplished my study goals?

⟹ Note: Re-do this checklist every three weeks to check your progress!

Study Buddy Activity

Show each other your schedules. Talk about your ways of managing your time well. Discuss how it feels to do so many things by the clock. Discuss what it feels like to be both a self-starter and a self-stopper. Share one thing that you do to just "get by" yet feel good about.

Talk with each other about your study habits. Find out what your study areas at home are like. Talk about how you handle distractions. Compliment each other for efforts and progress.

Chapter 7

How to Get
High Grades on Tests

Do you know that the best way to prepare for exams is to make and take practice tests?

Do you know that if you skip past a hard item during a test that you will often know the answer when you come back to it later?

Do you know that during an examination you can ask an instructor about test items?

Do you know that writing comments on tests is an effective way to reduce test anxiety?

How to Get High Grades on Tests

An examination is a series of questions you must answer. This means that your grades are determined by your ability to answer questions, not by how much the instructor likes you.

To get a high grade on a test you must be able to answer the questions asked by your instructor. That is why we emphasize looking for possible exam questions every time you read your textbook or course notes.

Do you see how this works? If you want to get high grades on your exams, spend your study time writing examination questions based on your textbook, class notes, and reading assignments. Then you take practice tests, ones that you created, covering predictable test items.

It is an inefficient use of your time to prepare for exams by reading, underlining, and rereading their lecture notes and texts. No instructor conducts an exam by asking you to read your notes or textbook to him or her. Your instructors ask you to answer questions based on their lecture notes, readings, and the textbook. The point is obvious:

IIIII➤ To do well on tests, devote your study time to making and taking practice tests!

Make Practice Tests

Imagine that you are the instructor and have to write some questions that will test the class on the material covered. When you do this for each course you will be amazed at how closely your test will be to the one your instructor creates.

If you ever played an instrument in a concert or played on an athletic team you spent many hours rehearsing and practicing. Preparation for exams is the same. You prepare for exams by taking practice exams.

Write the Kind of Questions That Will Be On the Exam

What sorts of questions should you use? The same kind of questions your instructor will ask. Remember what we said earlier, successful students begin a course asking *when* tests will be given and *what kind* they will be.

Will the test be multiple-choice? True-false? Short or long essay? A combination of these? Write your practice tests using the same kinds of questions.

Practicing the same kind of test items you will be required to answer in a test situation helps you relax. It builds your confidence. You feel less tension about tests. You know you have studied the right questions, and you sleep better knowing you've studied correctly.

Other Sources of Exam Questions

Textbooks and *lecture notes* are your best sources of questions, but there are other sources as well. They include the following:

Old Exams

You can look at past exams without feeling guilty. It is not cheating to do this. Old exams show you what an instructor thinks is the most important information students should know.

By looking at old exams you may find out:

1. Does the instructor repeat favorite questions every year?
2. Do test questions come primarily from lecture notes, the text, or from a variety of sources?
3. Does the instructor prefer multiple-choice, short-answer, true-false, or essay questions?

Student Manuals

The student manual written to accompany a textbook is an excellent source of exam questions. Student manuals contain true-false, multiple-choice, fill-in, and short essay questions. Even if your exam will be made up of questions that differ in style, the manual questions are still valuable.

> ▶ Note: *There may be a student manual for your textbook even if the instructor did not adopt it for the course.* Inquire about this. If a student manual exists, you can

purchase it through the bookstore or directly from the publisher. It can be worth it's weight in gold!

Other Students

Fellow students can be an excellent source of test questions. You can talk with students who have taken the course in past semesters to get information about the types of questions to expect.

Your Instructor:

Don't overlook asking your instructor for information about subjects and topics emphasized on the exam. As we said earlier, most instructors are happy to tell you what material they think is especially important. Some instructors will let you look at old tests. It won't hurt to ask questions such as:

- Will the test be objective, essay, or fill in the blank? Will it be a short, 20-item, true-false quiz? A 60-item multiple-choice test? A long essay test?
- How much time will be allotted?
- What proportion of the test will be based on lecture, readings, and the textbook?

Create a Folder with Practice Tests

Start each course with a plan. Read ahead in the textbook before class. Take accurate lecture notes. Then as soon as possible, convert the information in your lecture notes and corresponding textbook chapters into questions.

Write your practice test questions on sheets of paper separate from your lecture notes. If you use 3x5 cards, place the question on one side and the answer on the other.

How to Quiz Yourself

1. Create a practice test from the questions you've been developing from textbook chapters, lecture notes, and other sources.

2. Take your practice test without referring to your books or notes. (Keep the answers hidden!)
3. If you are not sure of the answer to an item, try to guess. Make up answers as if you were in a real testing situation, trying to earn at least partial credit.
4. After you complete your practice test, check the accuracy of your answers.
5. Revise any test questions that need to be written differently.

This easy procedure lets you quiz yourself quickly. You look at your questions, give your answers, and then check to see if your answers were accurate.

Using your study time in this way creates a growing file of questions and answers that you are confident you could answer on an instructor's exam. When an exam is scheduled you don't have to pour over lecture notes and textbook chapters. Your folder of questions and answers or their stacks of question cards and quiz themselves. You could even show these to your instructor and get a view on how good your questions are.

Another way to take practice tests is to have a friend or family member quiz you. Later, when you feel ready, get together with several classmates and quiz each other.

Do you have to drive a distance to get to the college? Here's how one student takes advantage of the time in her car:

> Besides doing 3x5 cards I record the questions on cassette tapes. I do a lot of driving. I play the tapes while I'm in the car. Hearing a question and saying the answer out loud helps. When I record the tapes I put on enough questions to make up about 15 minutes. Then I record about 15 minutes of music, changing back and forth between the two. For me the best music has a lively beat and no words, Bolero, Angel's Crossing etc.

Practice Tests Reduce Test Anxiety in All Subjects

Making and taking practice tests will eliminate the need for last minute cramming and greatly reduce exam panic. Short practice tests, taken every several days, will let you master small amounts of information each week.

This method helps reduce anxiety in math and science courses. Success in every course comes from frequent self-testing on the kinds of items that will be on instructor's exams. This method creates a feeling of familiarity and mastery even on math and science quizzes.

Before a mid-term or final exam, compile a comprehensive practice test made up of sample questions from your weekly tests. You'll be pleasantly surprised at how much easier it is to pass your final practice test when you have been taking weekly tests.

IIII➤ Remember: To reduce test anxiety, keep taking practice tests!

The Advantages of Practice Tests

Predicting exam questions is the most useful technique you can use for learning the important concepts covered in your courses. As amazing as it may seem, students who write test questions and take weekly practice tests spend *less time studying and get better grades!*

You also remember what you learn much better than when you cram for exams. The research by psychologists shows that people remember material better when they review and rehearse it.

> Some instructors will use test questions you write—especially well-written multiple choice or true-false items. It never hurts to ask the instructor if he or she would like to see questions you've written. Be sure to include chapter and page references, and mark the correct alternative. What a boost to sit down to a test and see *your* questions on it!—MK

The effectiveness of this study method has been proven over and over with thousands of students. This method helps you learn each subject quickly, get high grades, and obtain an excellent education. Your success in life is not determined by your course grades. It is a matter of what you know and what you can do. When you go to a dental hygienist to have your teeth cleaned, do you ask "What grades did you receive in school?" Probably not. You select professional services on the basis of what people know and can do.

How to Take Tests

General Guidelines
1. Read the instructions carefully. Glance at the entire exam to see where you'll earn the most points. Get a picture of how the test is laid out.
2. Look to see if answering questions that will be easy for you will earn as many points as the more difficult questions. If so, complete the easy questions first. After answering them you'll have more confidence, and you will be able to pass on to the more difficult questions. Do not start with the most difficult questions, get stuck on them, and then panic when you begin to run out of time.
3. Read each question carefully to grasp exactly what it is asking you to do. If the stem of the question says "What is an argument against...," then respond as requested. *Do exactly what the instructor requests!*
4. When you find an extremely difficult question or one you don't understand, move on to easier questions. Come back later to the ones you skipped. This reduces anxiety, saves time, and lets your subconscious mind search for the answer while you think about other items. Expect the answer to come to just as you do when trying to recall a person's name. Skipping past hard items is also practical because sometimes you find a clue to the answer in questions that follow.

Recognition Tests

There are two kinds of tests, tests that require you to *recognize* the right answer and tests that require you to *recall* the right answer from memory and write it down. Multiple-choice, true-false, and matching items are tests of recognition.

> Ⅲ▶ Tip: Many tests are given by using a scantron card for the answers. This makes grading the test easier but if you are in a hurry or under stress, it is easy to get on the wrong number for the answer. To avoid this problem use a ruler or straight edge of another paper to line your marked answers and check your number from time to time.

Read recognition questions carefully, but answer them quickly. If the answer is not immediately obvious to you, put a mark by the item and come back to it later. Never leave a question unanswered, unless there is a penalty for guessing.

You may have heard an instructor or some expert say to never change answers on a test. That is not good advice. Research shows that a much larger number of students gain by changing answers than the number of students who lose points by changing answers. Be careful, of course, about changing answers, but your second thought, *if you have prepared well*, has a good chance of being correct. After the tests are handed back, check to see how many times answers you changed were right.

Multiple-Choice Questions. When you answer a multiple-choice question, eliminate the incorrect alternatives first. This saves time and increases your chance of determining the right answer.

Pay close attention to key words and phrases such as "*According to* Freud…." or "Which is *not*…."

Go through the test rapidly, answering questions you know you know. Next, go back to those that you skipped the first time. Before handing in your exam go back to see if you read each item correctly. Be alert to questions that say "always, never, or only." There are few absolutes in life or on tests.

Additional Multiple-Choice Test Taking Tips:
• Put your name on the answer sheet!
• Read directions carefully before answering anything.

- When requested to choose the "best" answer, read them all very carefully.
- Read all options before answering.
- When undecided, read each answer with the question.
- Watch for clues to complete the sentence in the correct grammar.
- If you really do not have a clue, choose the longest answer.
- The second and third choices are more often correct than first and last choices.

Matching Questions. Read the directions for matching questions very carefully. If the instructions say "Match those that are opposite from each other," you'll kick yourself later if you matched similar items.

Identify the easy matches first. This reduces the chance of errors on more difficult matches.

> Tip: Count the number of items in each column to see if they are equal. Cross off each item as you use it *unless* you may use it more than once.

True-False Questions. Don't waste time puzzling over true-false questions. They are usually the first items on a test with different kinds of recognition questions. Unfortunately, some students waste lots of time on several true-false questions. If an answer isn't obvious, move on to other questions. One or two true-false items aren't worth that many points. Besides, the answer may become apparent later in the test as you answer other items.

> Tip: True/False tests frequently have more true answers than false. Unless you are penalized for incorrect answers, guess. *Do not leave blanks*. You have a 50/50 chance of being right.

Recall Tests

There are three types of tests of recall: long essays, short written answers, and fill-in items.

IIII➤ If an instructor says it is a *blue book* examination, you must go to the bookstore and purchase a thin book filled with lined pages that has a blue cover. It was designed specifically for essay examinations.

Long Essay Questions. Take a little time to outline your essay before you start writing. When you have made sure you will cover the most important points you will be more confident and relaxed. Remember that the purpose of the essay is to demonstrate your knowledge and understanding.

A well-written essay usually includes the following:

1. **Introduction.** Briefly describe the most important questions or present the main issues. Tell the reader what you are going to say and why.
2. **Use headings and subheadings.** Use headings for each major point or issue. Use subheadings every few paragraphs. Subheadings give the reader a quick understanding of the way you have organized your answer. (Notice how the headings and subheadings in this chapter show how the information is organized.)
3. **Demonstrate Critical Thinking.** Every field has conflicting views, findings, and interpretations. Your ability to present conflicting views demonstrates a much higher level of mastery and critical thinking about a subject. If your life experience gives you reservations about major views in the field, then say so.
4. **Give examples.** Illustrate your points with examples. They demonstrate that you really know what you are taking about.
4. **Provide Definitions** Show that you know what a term or concept means by giving its definition. Remember, the purpose of the test is for you to demonstrate depth of learning.
5. **Summarize.** Tell the reader what you have said. Be careful, however, to not include any new examples or information in the summary.
6. **Edit for clarity.** After you have finished writing, look through your essay to make certain you answered the

important questions. Look for careless mistakes. Edit your answers and clarify your statements.

▶ Note: To get yourself started on an essay question, it can help to ask yourself what are the important social, historical, psychological, economic, or physical aspects of this question.

Short-Answer Tests. A short answer test given during a typical 50 minute class period may contain from 20 to 40 items. Such tests usually say to:

- Summarize the main findings of....
- Define the terms and concepts listed below.
- State the main criticisms against....
- Identify the parts in the picture:
- Briefly describe two arguments in favor of....
- List the factors leading up to....
- Name the basic steps to follow in....
- Explain why....

Your answers on short-answer tests will usually be phrases and incomplete sentences. You will not be asked to write long paragraphs so do not study that way. The instructor wants an easy to read list of phrases and brief statements.

▶ A helpful tip: Before you start writing answers, write some of the information you memorized on the back of the exam.

When Questions Puzzle You

What can you do with a question that stumps you? Skip it until the end of the test. While answering other items, you will probably recall some information related to the answer. Before turning in your exam write down *anything* that demonstrates some learning. Do not leave an answer blank. It gives an instructor a negative impression. If you can't figure out the exact answer, you can probably come close.

Nervous? Write Comments About the Test

If your heart is pounding, your palms sweating, and you start to feel overwhelmed, imagine the following statement at the top of the test: "Feel free to write comments about the test items."

Research by psychologist Wilbert J. McKeachie, an expert on teaching and learning, discovered that students who received examinations with the "Feel free to write comments...." statement printed at the top of tests, did better on the test than students who did not. He found that it did not matter if students actually wrote anything about the test or not! The mere presence of the statement improved the scores of many students. This means that if you feel anxious or nervous or have fears of failing, it will help to write comments in the side or back of the test.

You Can Ask Questions During the Exam

Exam questions are not always clear. Instructors know that. Many times they create exam questions in a hurry late at night and sometimes a question is not worded well. That is why many instructors will talk with you about a test question during the exam.

If, even though you studied well, there is still a question you don't understand, go up to the instructor and ask about it. Say "I don't remember this material from the lecture or the text. Where was this information presented?" Or, "there are several correct answers to this item, which one do you want?"

You have nothing to lose by asking for some hints. The instructor will not give you the answer, but may remind you where the information was located in the textbook.

What You Gain From These Test-Taking Methods

Students who use the methods described in this chapter:

- usually receive high grades on tests.
- earn more points for answers than predicted.
- feel confident and relaxed during tests.
- seldom leave out important information.

- complete exams in time available.
- seldom misread the test questions or answer questions incorrectly.
- do not waste time on questions that stump them.
- do not put wrong or irrelevant information in answers.
- get more points on written items that let them "pad" their answers.
- seldom develop exam panic.
- get higher grades in their courses.
- demonstrate to the instructor that they have mastered the course content.
- sleep well the night before the exam!

How to Calculate Your Grade Point Average

You will probably learn about your grade in each course before the college sends you your grade report. If you don't want to wait, here is the method used for converting your course grades into a number called the Grade Point Average:

A = 4 grade points for each course hour
B = 3 grade points for each course hour
C = 2 grade points for each course hour
D = 1 grade point for each course hour
F = no points

To calculate your GPA, list how many credit hours each course was worth and the grade for each course. Multiply the credit hours for each course by the grade's value. Then add up both columns and divide the grade points by the credit hours:

Course	Credit Hours	Grade	Grade Point
Psychology	3	C	2 x 3 = 6
English	3	A	4 x 3 = 12
Biology	4	B	3 x 4 = 12
History	3	B	3 x 3 = 9
	13 hours		grade points = 39

Grade Point Average = 39 ÷ 13 = 3.0

Each term you add the new total of all your college credit hours and divide that number by the total of all your college grade points. By the end of your second year, for example, what would your GPA be if you had taken 120 credit hours and earned 420 grade points?

Action Review: Checklist for Success in Preparing for and Taking Tests

☐ At the start of each course do I find out what kind of examination the instructor will use?

☐ After each class do I write and then quiz myself on possible test questions?

☐ Do I practice taking the tests I create every week?

☐ When I take tests, do I use the methods recommended in this chapter?

Study Buddy Activity

Talk with each other about taking tests. How do you feel and what do you do the night before? Do you feel confident? Get a good night's sleep? How do you feel on the way to the test? What is your self-talk like when you walk into the room and sit waiting for the tests to be passed out? Is taking tests similar to other life experiences you have had? Share practical tips with each other about what you do to handle your nervousness about tests

After you have taken tests, show each other the test results. Talk about how well you handled yourself and what you could do better next time. Compare the practice exams that you made up with the actual test. Find out if you were on target or not. Your study buddies will tell you!

Chapter 8

How to Write Excellent Papers

Do you know your starting point when writing papers should be, "What questions am I trying to answer in this paper?"

Do you know the ability to write excellent papers may depend on how well you know how to use the library?

Do you know which librarian to talk to when you need help?

Do you know the difference between a barely acceptable paper and an excellent one is determined by your ability to revise and rewrite?

The Secret to Writing "A" Papers

You do not have to have a high IQ to write a term paper that gets an "A." All you have to do is:

- always keep in mind you are writing your paper for one person, your instructor.
- select a topic interesting for you and one that your instructor feels is important.
- make your paper a series of answers to important questions.
- present contrasting views or positions to demonstrate your capacity for critical thinking.
- show your instructor your outline for your paper before putting a lot of work into it.

Interview Your Instructor

Select two potential topics for your paper. A good way to investigate a research topic is to consult an encyclopedia. The *Encyclopedia Britannica* is an excellent resource. If it covers a subject, it will provide you with a comprehensive summary and the important viewpoints about it.

Make a list of important questions and issues for each topic. Work up a one page outline of what you would do with each topic.

Meet with your instructor before you start writing your paper. Interview the instructor to find out which topic the instructor feels would be the best one for you to write about. Ask the instructor if there are important references you should look at and refer to in the paper. Ask the instructor "What important questions and critical issues should I cover in the paper?" Listen well. The instructor will probably tell you exactly what he or she will want to see in the paper. You make things much easier for yourself when you do this!

Start With Questions

Begin your research by listing specific questions you intend to answer in your paper. If you aren't certain how to start, go to the library and talk to one of the reference librarians. They can help you find sources of information you don't know about. That is what their job is. Use their expertise.

The Computer Can Do Your Search

Once you have a list of questions, start looking for answers. Begin in the college library. In most college libraries your search for information sources will start with a computer terminal. Catalogs are now on-line, and the old card catalog or microfiche are rapidly becoming tools of the pre-computer age. The on-line computer system records availability of books and journals and even allows you to reserve materials that are in other locations. If you are unsure of how to use the computer terminals, ask the librarian for help. The one thing that has not changed is that the librarian is a very helpful person.

Libraries have their index on computers and you can access information by author, subject, and title. You'll probably want to start with the subject index.

Use your imagination when searching the subject index. Look under every topic you can think of. The abstracts of articles are a quick way to research relevant data. Make notes of book titles and authors, and always write down the complete call number of the book. The *call number* is the library's code number that tells you exactly where the book is shelved.

> Note: When you see the statement "reserve" or "reserve desk" by a book, you will *not* find the book in the open shelves. An instructor has had the book placed in a special reserve section where it can be signed out for a limited amount of time, usually a couple of hours to overnight.

Periodical Sources

The most recent information on a subject appears in professional journals long before it is written up in books. Look in the library's periodical index for titles of journals that would contain articles related to your topic.

Be sure to look under "Journal," "American," and "National" in the alphabetical listings. The journals of professional groups are often titled *The Journal of...*, *The American...*, or *National Society of...*, etc.

When you write down call numbers for books and journals, you will notice that the books and journals with information about your topic will be located in two or three places in the library. Then when you go to these locations in the stacks, you will discover other useful books and journals.

From the journal articles you learn about books to research. From the books you will learn about journals that focus on your topic most frequently.

Skim articles and books first to get a general orientation. When you find useful data or passages you may want to quote in your paper, record the name and date of the publication, the title of the article or chapter, and write down or photocopy the quote exactly as it was printed. It is very frustrating when you can't remember which author you quoted or which statement in your notes is your own summary. Libraries have photocopiers available. You will save time using them.

Be sure to look at *The Reader's Guide to Periodical Literature.* It lists articles published in popular magazines. Don't discount magazines as a source of information, because some scientific research is published directly in them. Besides, the information is less technical than in professional journals and books.

If you do not find the information you need in your library, your librarian can search local, national and even international sources on the information highway to obtain for you the most up-to-date references.

> ⬛⬛▶ Note: Libraries have greatly expanded their video and audio selections. If you find you learn easier by watching and listening, consider using these convenient resources.

Search for Answers
You'll discover that by having questions in mind that you want to answer, you can quickly cut through the massive amount of

material that could otherwise distract you. By reading to answer your questions, you avoid the needless loss of hours wondering how much you should include in your paper.

Expect New Questions

In the process of answering questions, new questions may arise. You may find that as you do your research you need to change the original questions in some way or add some new ones.

Writing a Rough Draft

Now that you've gathered your information, it is time to write a rough draft about your questions and the answers you found. Write your first draft quickly. Don't waste time trying to make your first draft your final draft.

Start by presenting your questions and explaining why they are important.

Write the answers to each question. Make your point and back it up with examples. Answers to questions are more believable when they are clear and well supported.

Quote from your sources. Brief quotes, facts, and figures have more effect than personal impressions, opinions, or generalizations. Give exact references for your quotes and facts.

Arrange your answers so that they connect in a logical way. Connect them by saying, showing, explaining, or demonstrating how they are related to each other.

Demonstrate Critical Thinking

Very few instructors want you to parrot back exactly what some authority has said. They want you to show that you can think intelligently about the subject. They want you to demonstrate critical thinking.

How do you show critical thinking? By presenting contrasting or conflicting perspectives. Don't pick one viewpoint and present it as right while others are wrong. Present the strengths and weaknesses of one perspective and the strengths and weaknesses of a contrasting perspective.

Your life experience gives you an advantage over

younger students here. You know there are always two sides to a story. Present both sides plus your own ideas about what this all means.

Summarize and Draw Conclusions

At the end of your paper summarize the main points and add two or three conclusions. The summary explains what you have done in your paper, justifies your conclusions, and demonstrates critical thinking. Be sure to check your summary against the introduction to your paper. Do they match? If not, revise your introduction.

Listen to Your Paper

The best way to quickly determine if your paper makes sense is to read it out loud. When you read it aloud, a rough sentence structure or a statement that does not make sense will be very apparent. After reading your paper aloud to yourself, consider reading it aloud to a study buddy or a classmate.

Correct Your Grammar and Spelling

Make sure that your spelling and grammar are accurate. Use a spell checker or a dictionary when in doubt. Have someone else proofread your paper. Few things bother instructors more than poor spelling and bad grammar. Instructors tend to give higher grades to papers clearly typed, grammatically correct, and free of spelling errors.

Consult Your Instructor

Make an appointment to go over your first draft with your instructor. Many instructors will give you good feedback about revising you will need to do if you want an "A."

Revise and Rewrite

The real writing of any paper, of course, takes place when you rewrite and edit your first draft. Most good papers require several revisions before achieving the final version.

During your rewriting, revising, and editing ask yourself:
- Have I clearly stated the questions my paper will answer?

- Are the questions I selected important to the topic and cover it well?
- Have I answered the questions effectively?
- Is my writing interesting to listen to?
- Have I corrected grammatical, punctuation, and spelling errors?
- Does my summary accurately cover the main points of my paper?
- Do my conclusions demonstrate critical thinking and cover what I learned in the process of writing the paper?

IIII▶ Note: If you feel the need for help with your writing, contact the English department. English departments usually run a writing skills center for non-English majors. It is worth looking into.

Caution: Do Not Plagiarize

Once in awhile, a student will copy passages from a book or magazine article and turn in the paper as his or her own work. Trying to pass off someone else's work as your own is called *plagiarism*. It rarely succeeds. A paper written by a student attempting to learn a subject is not the same as material written by an expert. Most instructors can tell when writing is not a student's own.

It is human to consider taking shortcuts, but plagiarizing is not worth the risk. Plagiarism is unethical and usually illegal.

IIII▶ It is also plagiarism to turn in a paper written by another student. This means you don't let a study buddy copy your work, you don't copy theirs, and you don't do their work for them.

Make Your Papers Look Good

If you want a top grade, produce a clean, sharp looking paper. Type or word process all your papers. Instructors prefer printed, easy to read papers because of their constant struggle to avoid eye strain. If you don't have keyboard skills, consider taking a class. It is one of the best self-improvement efforts you can make.

Many English departments have their composition courses conducted as computer labs, so you might want to take an English composition course right away. It is a good way to develop computer literacy if you are not familiar with computers.

Make your paper as professional looking as possible. Most instructors will accept papers printed by dot matrix printers if the ribbon is not too old. Use clean white paper. Double space the lines. Keep handwritten corrections on the final copy at a minimum.

Be sure to follow all directions your instructor gives for the way you should do footnotes, references, and other procedures. It is a waste of time and energy to devote hours to a paper only to have it returned as incomplete. *The consequences of failing to follow directions can be costly.*

A word to the wise: Hand in a paper you are proud of! If it were a business report that would affect your chances for a pay increase, would you submit it the same way?

> ⫸ Note: *Always* make a copy of your paper. The original could get damaged or lost. Play it safe. Keep a copy and be sure it is saved on a computer disk.

Action Review: Checklist for Success in Writing Papers and Using Your Library

❑ Do I write papers using the question and answer format?

❑ Have I asked the reference librarian for suggestions about where to look for information?

❑ Do I use the card catalog, microfiche, or on-line system to track down good reference sources?

❑ Do I get up-to-date information from professional journals?

❑ Are my quotes and references accurate?

☐ When my first draft is completed, do I ask the instructor to look it over and give me suggestions for improvement?

☐ Do I check for correct grammar and spelling?

☐ Do my papers reflect my ability for critical thinking?

☐ Am I proud of what I hand in?

Study Buddy Activity

Talk about what you know about your college library. What tips do you have for each other about using the on-line system? If none of you know, then arrange for a demonstration by one of the librarians.

When you are developing ideas for papers, bounce topic ideas and key questions back and forth. Choose topics that interest you. It helps to feel enthusiastic about your topic.

After you have produced your first rough draft, show it to the others. Read each other's papers out loud and ask questions. Help each other create contrasting perspectives that demonstrate critical thinking. Take turns giving each other both suggestions and appreciation.

REVIEW AND PREVIEW

The first two sections of this book covered basic information on how to get started in college and how to succeed in your courses. By now you have learned that your college provides helpful services and assistance on each of the areas covered in the first eight chapters. If you find yourself struggling with any of these challenges go to talk to someone in the college counseling department. The people there are friendly and very good at problem solving student difficulties. They will help you stick with your education plan.

The first two sections covered important academic skills, the next two sections cover important life skills. Without good life skills, you reduce your chances of getting the education you desire and the career you seek.

In some classes, for example, you will be required to team up with a few other students to do a project. Part of your grade will be based on how well your team does. As a member of a class team, as with a work place team, you must deal with differences in personalities, working styles, and cultural backgrounds. In the next section you will find guidelines for understanding and successfully resolving predictable conflicts with others.

Do you handle pressure and constant change well? Select and transition into a new career easily? Enjoy working for an employer that does not provide job descriptions? Are you flexible and resilient? The fourth section shows how to develop the inner strengths needed for thriving in a world of non-stop change.

Knowing Yourself and Others

Chapter 9

Learning Styles and Teaching Styles: How to Influence Instructors

Do you know that your studying and learning will be easier if you understand your learning style?

Do you know that difficulties in a course can stem from a conflict between a student's learning style and the instructor's teaching style?

Do you know you can improve the teaching you get?

Do you know it is possible to overcome a poor start in a course and get a good final grade?

Learning Styles: They Can Help or Hinder

Researchers wanting to understand all aspects of success in college asked: "Why do some students do well with one instructor but not another?" Their research uncovered a simple truth about academic life:

> *The way an instructor teaches will not fit with the way some students learn.*

Other research looked at why students show wide differences in the time of day and the circumstances best for learning. This research identified an important truth about studying and learning:

> *The ideal learning circumstances for one student may not be good for another student.*

Research findings and experience have identified the following important differences in how people learn.

External versus Internal Learning Styles

Psychologists have done extensive research on an important personality difference between people. It is called the "external and internal locus of control."

Externally oriented students believe information when it comes from an authority or expert. Information or suggestions from other sources aren't trusted as accurate.

If your instructor enjoys being an expert who tells the class exactly what to learn, the better an externally orientated student will do with this type of instructor. If you desire clear guidelines from an instructor, but take a course from someone who provides little direction, you may flounder.

Some students who want to listen to an authority react negatively to classes where the instructor encourages discussion and encourages students to develop their own views and answers. These students protest, "I didn't pay good money to sit and listen to a bunch of uninformed people express their opinions. I can get that in the cafeteria." This attitude is legitimate, but it is also narrow minded.

The word *education* means to "draw out of." It does not mean "shovel into." A good education does not give you a diploma for learning how to seek out an expert for any question you have. A good education teaches you to think for yourself. It teaches you to ask questions and how to find the answers on your own.

Self-motivated, internally oriented students appreciate an instructor who allows them freedom to follow their own paths. Such students get upset with instructors who tell them exactly what they must learn, and in what way. For them, too much course structure is abrasive. They feel handicapped more than helped. Such reactions are legitimate and narrow minded.

Being Both Internal and External in Learning

Students who get the most out of school are able to follow the tightly-controlled steps used by some teachers and, at the same time, organize their own learning experiences when in a class taught by someone who gives few guidelines. Can you learn to do both?

Auditory versus Visual Styles

Have you ever noticed that you can tell a person something but it doesn't register unless you write it down for them? Or that someone might read a note you've left, but the message didn't get through to their brain? That is because people differ in how information gets into their consciousness.

Some people learn best by reading. They must see something before they believe it and remember it. Other people learn best by listening. Information doesn't stick well unless they hear it. Some people learn best by doing. What is your natural style?

- Do you prefer to listen to the radio or read newspapers for the news?

- Do you remember best what you read or what is said to you?

- Would you rather read what an expert has written on a

subject or hear the expert talk?

- When you purchase new equipment do you read the instruction manual carefully or do you rarely read manuals?

Based on your answers to these questions, which learning style do you tend to prefer? Auditory or visual?

Everyone learns both ways, of course. It is not an either/or situation. Yet the differences between people are sometimes extreme enough to cause problems. If you have a visual learning style, you operate mainly on the basis of what you read. You may have difficulty with an instructor who believes that telling people what to learn and know is sufficient.

Visual Learning Style

If you learn best visually, you may be in trouble with an instructor who doesn't use handouts, emphasizes class discussion, and doesn't write much on the blackboard. The solution with a verbally oriented instructor is to:

1. Take good notes on what the instructor and your classmates say. After class fill in sentences and compare notes with other students.

2. Ask the instructor for suggested articles or books that will let you read the information you need to understand better.

3. Consciously work at listening and remembering what the instructor says. TIP: One woman wrote to us saying that she types her lecture notes immediately after every class.

4. If you are confused about a point, ask the instructor to tell you again and write down what you hear.

5. Ask instructor if an outline of the lecture is available.

Auditory Learning Style

If you have an auditory style, you will probably do well with an instructor who says everything to learn and do. You may have difficulty with a visually-oriented instructor. Such an instructor hands out a written statement about what to do to pass the course without discussing it, and assigns textbook material and outside readings that are never discussed in class.

The solution, if you have an auditory style in a class taught by a visually-oriented instructor is to:

1. Find classmates who will tell you what they learned from the textbook readings.
2. Dictate the main points from the reading assignments and handouts onto cassette tape and then listen to the tapes.
3. Consciously work at improving your ability to acquire information visually. (Note: For professional help, go to the reading improvement center or the office of disabilities.)

Indications of a Tactile Learner:

Some people are strongly oriented to make physical connections with the world around them. Neither reading nor hearing has as much impact as doing something with the subject being studied. You may be a tactile learner if you:

- Put physical work before studying
- Find it hard to sit for long periods—want to be moving
- Want to say "Show me and let me DO it."
- Like lab or shop work. Lectures are hard to sit through.
- Move a lot while learning, i.e. swing foot, twist hair, tap pencils.

What can you do to keep lectures and reading interesting? Go visit places where the course material is being used in real-life settings. Draw what you are learning. Be creative about ways to get physical with the subject.

Understanding Differences in Temperament

Isabel Myers and her mother, Katheryn Briggs, developed a test to measure four dimensions of temperament identified by Carl Jung. Myers-Briggs type tests are probably the most popular personality tests given these days because of many benefits gained from seeing how differences in temperament explain misunderstandings between people.

This means that differences in *how* you and an instructor think are more important than differences in *what* you think. Here is how the four temperaments influence your learning style:

Extroversion versus Introversion

Instructors and students vary widely in how friendly they want to be and how much emotional distance they need to have. A friendly, extroverted instructor enjoys after-class contact with students. He or she will ask students to coffee or out for pizza. If you are similarly friendly, you will have a great year.

If you are a more introverted person, however, you may suffer from too much personal attention and closeness. You would much rather have a quiet, more distant instructor who respects your need to be left alone. Such an instructor understands how embarrassing it is to be openly praised for getting a high score on an exam.

On the other hand, if you are an extroverted person with a more introverted instructor, you may find it puzzling to have him or her pulling away from you after class. After all, what are instructors for if not to be available for students? Yet your desire to be friendly may cause the instructor to stare at you and make excuses to get away. After that, you may feel avoided.

When it come to studying, the introverted person needs a private, quiet place where everyone stays away. The extroverted person likes to study in the kitchen, in a student lounge, or with classmates. If you grew up in a large family you may study best in a noisy place with lots of people around. Experiment with locations to see what works best for you. Don't hesitate to tell friends, relatives, and classmates with temperaments different than yours what you need.

Thinking versus Feeling

Descriptions of this dimension of temperament match up closely with left-brain/right-brain research findings. The left brain is where the speech center develops in most humans. The left brain is where you remember words, use logic, and think analytically. It gives you your ability to think rationally and unemotionally. The left brain thinks in a linear fashion. It is time oriented.

The right brain carries your memory for music. You think visually, emotionally, and irrationally in the right brain. It is the source of creativity and intuition. Right-brain thinking follows emotional logic. Using it, you can visualize and think in patterns jumping from one spot in a pattern to another without apparent logic or reason.

If you tend to be left-brained, you will be well matched to an instructor who gives you thorough, unemotional listings of facts, data, analytic explorations, hypotheses, logic, evidence, numbers, definition of terms, and rational conclusions.

If you tend to be left-brained and get an instructor who teaches in a right-brained way, you may find the course to be a bewildering experience. You may experience the instructor as weird, too emotional, disorganized, and a bit nutty.

If you tend to be right-brained with a left-brained teacher, the course will be painful for you. You'll feel like a thirsty person handed a glass of water only to find it is filled with sand.

IIII➤ To resolve personality conflicts such as these, avoid indulging in the attitude "If only other people would change, my world would be a better place for me."

When you have a mismatch, you can try to find someone (perhaps even the instructor) who will translate the material into a form you understand better. More important, however, make an effort to gain more use of your other brain.

The situation may not be easy at first, but it does give you a chance to add another dimension to yourself. And isn't this why you're in school?

You do not have to give up your more natural and preferred way of thinking, feeling, and talking. What you can do is add more to what you already have. We'll get into more of this in the chapter on the survivor personality.

Sensation versus Intuition
Sensation oriented people are guided by experience. Intuitive people like fantasy, they are creative dreamers. According to David Keirsey and Marylin Bates, authors of *Please*

Understand Me, differences on this dimension cause the widest gulf between people.

The sensation oriented student is practical, wanting facts and evidence. An intuitive instructor can fill the lecture hour with hypothetical explanations, theories, concepts, and a long list of views held by others.

A sensation oriented instructor gives practical instructions on what to do. An intuitive student wants to know what the underlying theories and concepts are, and asks "but what if?"

What to do about this sort of conflict? Stretch your understanding. Ask for what you need. Try to minimize the judging dimension of the next pair of traits.

Judging versus Perceiving

If you remember Archie Bunker from the television series *All in the Family*, you have seen an excellent example of the judging temperament. Such people make up their minds quickly. They judge others and situations as good or bad, right or wrong.

The perceiving style is to observe without judgment. Such people can watch world events, movies, and sports events without taking sides or having an opinion.

A judgmental style instructor believes the purpose for being in college is to work hard to become qualified for an occupation where hard work will get you ahead. The instructor works hard, expects the same from every student, and privately judges students as good ones or bad ones.

A perceiving instructor looks for ways to make learning fun, tries to minimize office work, and sees all students as learners. This instructor is frustrating for a judging style student who wants serious homework and wants to know how he or she compares to the other students.

▮▮▶ Note: If you want to take a Myers-Briggs type assessment of temperaments, check with the counseling office or careers center. Many colleges have a software program that lets you take the test and get a printout of your scores.

Practical Suggestions

What do you do when a teacher is less than ideal? Do you get distressed? Complain?

By now we hope you have realized that finding a really good match between yourself and an instructor does not happen all the time. As an alternative to feeling like a victim and blaming the instructor for your poor grade, we have the following suggestions:

1. Before registration ask around to find out about various instructors. If you have a choice between instructors, you'll know which one to choose.
2. Try to get as much out of every course as you can, regardless of who your instructor is or how much the teaching style does not fit your preferred learning style. Be open to try a new way of learning.
3. When you have a difficulty understanding what is happening in a course, make an appointment to talk with the instructor. Be prepared to ask for what you want.
4. If you still have problems, go to the office or center that teaches studying and reading skills. The specialists there can be very helpful.

Learn to Appreciate Human Differences

We humans are all born with different temperaments and different ways of functioning in life. That is simply the way things work. When you experience conflicts with others at school, at work, or in your family, question your attitudes about other people. If you experience an irritating difference, use that as an opportunity to learn more about human nature. You might as well, because you won't change other people by criticizing them!

The better you know yourself, the more skillfully you will manage your learning style and the easier it will be to succeed in college!

How to Influence Your Instructors

Give Feedback to Instructors

You can influence how your instructors teach. When an instructor does something you appreciate, let them know right away. Don't wait until you are given a course evaluation at the end of the course. After class compliment them or hand them a note. When you and the other students praise good teaching, you'll get more of what you like and less of what you don't like.

If you want to tell an instructor there is something that needs to be improved, give a specific example of what you don't like and what you would like.

How to Turn a Bad Situation Around

So here you are, you totally blew the mid-term, got a D on your project and could end up with a D or F in the course. Is your situation hopeless? Not at all. You can often salvage a bad grade.

Make an appointment to talk with your instructor. *Go with a plan!* If you did poorly on the mid-term or even on the final, ask to take the make-up exam. Ask for a chance to show that you do know the material. Ask if you can write an extra paper or rewrite the project you threw together the night before it was due. Explain why you wish to do better. Instructors are much more inclined to give students a chance when they admit they have done poorly and want to turn things around.

Even if the instructor says you cannot take the test to change your grade, ask to take it anyway to see for yourself if you can do better. Assuming that you will get a better score, this will have a psychological effect on the instructor later.

Most instructors will give you a chance. A bad grade is not inevitable unless you allow it to be. A sincere request for another chance, a specific plan about what you will do, and commitment to do it will influence most instructors.

> IIII➤ WARNING: Do not just walk away from a class
> where you are doing poorly. Officially drop the class.
> A failing grade turned in at the end of the course
> becomes part of your permanent school record.

One of my early learning experiences involved messing up on a mid-term exam. There was no make-up exam. I felt desperate. I wrote out three questions that could be used as the basis for writing long essays. Then I went to the instructor and asked if I could get extra credit for researching and answering one or more of the three questions. I said I would write my answers in the form of a paper using information from outside the textbook. I was delighted when he agreed to my request. I ended up with a B in the course. The results would have been different if I had not done the extra credit work.—MK

Consider Taking an Incomplete

If you anticipate a bad grade in a course because you have not been able to get all of the work in, and you want to earn a good grade, then consider asking the instructor to submit an *incomplete* on the grade sheet. All colleges have policies for allowing students to complete course work after the course is over. At most colleges you have at least a year.

Courses Can be Repeated

You can change the past if you want to. If you get a low grade in an important subject you can repeat the course to replace a low grade with a higher one. Repeating a course is always an option.

Instructors Are Human!

You will have great instructors, average instructors, and some that you believe are teaching only because they couldn't hold a job out in the real world. The point is that instructors are human beings who vary in their teaching styles and who react just as you do to the way they are treated. You can influence the quality of the teaching you get.

Action Review: Identifying Differences Between Teaching and Learning Styles

❑ When I don't relate to the way an instructor teaches do I look to see if there is a conflict between my learning style and the instructor's teaching style?

❑ If any of the following are descriptive of me do I take steps to compensate for my natural style in classes with instructors with different styles?

external direction — internal direction
auditory — visual — tactile
extroverted — introverted
left brain (thinking) — right brain (feeling)
sensible — intuitive
judging — perceiving

❑ Have I examined my assumptions about instructors and developed a more realistic and tolerant attitude?

Action Project for Getting Better Teaching

1. Talk with several classmates about what you like for instructors to do. Make a list of specific actions you see as desirable.
2. Make a list of ways you could give positive feedback when an instructor does things you appreciate.
3. Let instructors know what you appreciate.

Study Buddy Activity

Talk about how conflicts between teaching styles and learning styles may be able to explain difficulties you have had with instructors in the past. Work with each other to develop a plan for handling future conflicts.

Discuss how the information in this chapter explains personality conflicts you've had at home or at work. Can you recognize any of your relatives, co-workers or managers in these descriptions?

Talk about some of your past experiences with good instructors and poor instructors. Talk about your teaching experiences as parents or managers. How easy is it? What feedback did you appreciate from people you tried to teach?

Chapter 10

Your Family and Friends: How to Gain Their Support and Encouragement

Do you feel guilty about doing something just for yourself?

Can you ask people for help when you need it?

Do you wonder if you will upset your family or your friends because you are going to school?

Do you know how to develop and follow a positive plan of action for getting the help and support you need?

Do you understand what it means to give high-quality time to others?

There's a Way, If You Will...

Your family and friends do not have to feel deprived by the extra time you spend in school. If mealtime conversation is filled with interesting conversational tidbits, if dreams of an exciting tomorrow are shared with those who are close, and they see a happier, more enthusiastic person, they will be glad for you.

You Can Make It Work

Making the pieces fit, maintaining relationships and school successfully takes time and planning. You will not find all the adjustments or solutions overnight. Fitting into a new role is never easy and it may take six months to a year before you and those close to you have made the transition.

Getting an education is the best insurance you can buy for a successful, secure future. Learning is a lifelong experience. Finding the right combination for relationships, work, and school can pay off big dividends in personal and professional satisfaction.

How to Gain the Support You Need

Here is a simple and effective way to get support, help, encouragement, and understanding from your family and friends:

1. Take some time privately to think about the support you need from others in your new role as a student.
2. Decide to seek that support.
3. Talk to the people whose support you are seeking. Explain why going to school is important to you. Ask what worries they might have and listen with understanding. Ask what positive feelings they have about your going back to school and what advantages they may see for themselves.
4. Be very specific in asking for the support you need— undisturbed time alone, encouragement, household chores done, etc.

5. Track positives with people. Reward any actions you regard as positive, helpful, or supportive with thanks and appreciation. Give others immediate feedback about what you like.

Plan Ahead
Think through what you want to talk about and what requests you will make. Select the best time to talk.

Taking night classes may mean that the family mealtime will be disrupted. If you are working full time and going to school part time, you will have less time together. Find out how they feel about this change and empathize with their concerns rather than telling them not to feel the way they do. Let them know that your time together is important to you.

If people are reluctant to talk about what is ahead, make some effort to get them to think about the months and years ahead. It is essential to keep the lines of communication open to avoid a big blowup someday at just the wrong time.

Don't assume the worst, you may be surprised!

> Before I started to school I sat down with the three teenage children who were still at home and talked with them about what changes might occur in their lives as a result of my commitment to school. The kids were wonderful! They encouraged me so heartily I should have been suspicious, but I wasn't....Years later, after they were out of high school, they told me they were eager to get me involved elsewhere so that they would have more freedom to come and go as they wanted! —MK

Let People Know What You Want
Students with families have requests such as these:

- I would like my three teenage children to do more housework, so that I will have more time for my studies.
- I'd like my husband and kids to fix dinner for themselves a couple of nights a week when I am at class.

- It would be nice to have my wife ask me about my courses and spend a little time talking about my experiences as a student.
- I'd appreciate being left alone to study three nights a week; that means not knocking on my door or interrupting to tell me about something on TV.

Why don't people get what they want? The answer is surprising. They usually have not asked.

Most of us were raised not to be selfish. Some selfishness is essential, however, when expressed in a way that is not demanding.

Most people report that once they have the courage to ask for support, they receive far more than they expected. Some students report that when they finally ask for what they want, the reply is "Why didn't you ask before? Sure, I'll be glad to do that!"

Getting Help at Home

Anyone who manages a home knows there are certain maintenance tasks that must be done—homework, or not. When dirty socks and underwear carpet the floor, it is time for some cooperation and delegation. Most children over the age of seven, and most partners, can learn to pick up, sort, and put the clothes in the washing machine.

Even a four-year-old can help fold clothes and put them away. To reverse an old quote, "Ask not what you can do for others, but what can they do for you!" As roles change, it is time to delegate responsibilities to other household members.

Have a meeting with the family each week to develop a chore schedule. On a piece of paper, list the jobs each person agrees to do and specify when it will be done. It helps to rotate the responsibility for developing the weekly list to others. Participate in the discussion, of course, but when you have someone else write down the various duties and place the list in a conspicuous place, it will seem less imposed by you.

Post your own weekly time schedule in a conspicuous place so that all can see where you will be and when. When members of your household see that Thursday evening from 7:30 to 9:00 is a study period, they will be more likely to leave you alone, especially *if you stick with your own schedule!*

IIII➡ TIP: Others will be less likely to interrupt or intrude during your study hours if you set aside specific times during the week for each important person.

Quality is Better Than Quantity
Reserve one solid hour each week for each important person. Others will be less demanding when they know they have their own special time with you. For example, talk with your daughter Cheryl about when she'd like her hour. Write "Cheryl's hour" in big letters on your schedule. Then make sure she gets her hour with you. Do not try to fit more than one person into the same hour. Make these hours very important to you. Avoid missing one or changing one if you possibly can.

Let the others decide what will be done during their hour. Self-esteem develops or is maintained by being in close contact with others, by being seen as unique, by feeling important, and from being able to influence the world. So don't plan this hour, let the person influence what you do together.

Be curious about what develops. Many people who have done this report that their personal relationships and contacts with family members improve significantly.

Working together on tasks at home can be important time together. As one sets the table, another scrubs the potatoes, someone unloads the dishwasher, and the microwave zaps the main course, each person talks about their day. Time for sharing is essential when you have to juggle work, home, and school. Sharing, caring, and doing the work together can all be done at the same time.

Use a Little Psychology

Thousands of experiments conducted by psychologists over the years have established the validity of a principle that affects the actions of others. The principle is:

▯▯▯▶ *Actions that are rewarded tend to increase.*

Consequently,

1. If you thank, compliment, and reward others for doing what is helpful to you they will do even more.
2. If you stop rewarding, they'll do less of what is helpful.

What rewards can you use? Here is a list of suggestions from adult students about things they've done:

- Express appreciation.
- Say "thank you."
- Buy or fix their favorite food for them.
- Give hugs and kisses.
- Give treats or little gifts.
- Be interested in their lives.
- Tell them about something interesting at school.
- Speak highly of them to others.
- Give them back rubs and neck massages.
- Let them feel that your success is their success.
- Ask what they would like from you.
- Leave nice notes for them; send cards.

When you speak clearly about what you would like from others and then follow up with "thank-you's" and rewards, you usually get results that exceed your expectations. Most people respond in very positive ways. In fact, you may be overwhelmed by all the love and support others show you.

Expect Surprises

Expect some surprises and be prepared to make some adjustments of your own when your life changes. Letting people do things their own way may be difficult at first, but a positive attitude and a sense of humor can pull you through.

In one family, for example, the children (grade-school age) volunteered to cook dinner one evening a week. They accepted full responsibility for shopping, cooking, and cleaning up afterward. Their mother said she assumed the meal would be done the way she always did it. She reported:

> The first time they "cooked" dinner they met me at the door all excited and led me to the dining room before I could take off my coat. I expected steaming plates with vegetables, salad, and so forth. When I walked in my eyes almost fell out of my head. Their idea of a great dinner was boiled hot dogs served on paper plates with a bottle of pop, a bag of potato chips, and Twinkies for dessert! I didn't know whether to collapse in hysterical laughter or lecture them on the right way to shop, cook, and serve a nutritious meal. I did neither. As I sat there eating a barely warm wiener, I told myself it wouldn't kill me to let them do it their way. I've had some interesting meals since then. Peanut butter sandwiches and pie aren't too bad. And the paper plates are real time and energy savers.

Things Don't Always Work Out

Some students find that their home situations do not get better. Some family members may become difficult. A partner may start to drink more or stay out late. Children may begin to get into trouble or have difficulty at school.

If anything this extreme takes place, it is important to seek professional advice and counseling. Get to know what services are available at the college. There are many experts you can talk to and a variety of sources of help. Other students can provide support and practical advice. Ask around and you are likely to discover that more good solutions are possible than you imagined.

They Need Emotional Support

It can be easy to forget that family and friends need some nurturing, too. An instructor once said to an over-achieving beginner, "When it comes to a choice of studying extra to get an A on the mid-term, working overtime, or taking your children to the zoo—take the kids to the zoo." A little attention in time saves resentment in the long run.

When you return to school, people close to you may react as though you are changing the rules on them. A change in your daily routines forces them to change theirs, and they may resist.

Adult students find the return easier if they are prepared for the mixed emotions that others may have about their changed roles. It helps to understand their feelings, and then help them see that your going back to school is good for them as well.

Bev had four children when she decided to return to school. Two seemed to adjust fine to the new schedule, but one daughter was getting more "mouthy" and her son said resentfully, "Why can't you be like other mommies and just stay home?"

The next term Bev scheduled classes so she could be at home when the children came home from school. She started a ten-minute contact time for each child where sharing the day and hugging and touching was made a priority when they first came home. The discipline and resentment problems disappeared.

It May Take a While
The more your family and friends have been dependent on you, the more difficult it will be for them to be more responsible for themselves. If you meet resistance, the change can be difficult. They may become upset and refuse to talk. They may accuse you of being selfish and of not caring about them.

There are many reasons for such reactions. A husband may secretly fear that if his wife becomes capable, educated, and employable, she may decide to leave. A wife may feel neglected having her husband work full time and then devote evenings and weekends to school. Your friends miss your calls.

Try to not let others make you feel guilty if they become upset. Let them know you understand their feelings but don't take too much responsibility for their unhappy reactions. Would you let a ten-year-old control how you drive or where you go? Are others better qualified to make decisions about your life than you are? Does your partner know your needs better than you do?

Hold true to your plan for yourself while you give others time to adjust to this new way of life. Let them know how important they are to you.

Develop a Plan and Be Positive

Going to school can solve problems. Try to use your returning to school as an opportunity to improve your relationship with your loved ones. Healthful relationships are based on people's supporting each other's growth and development, not dependence. Your returning to school could lead to deeper, closer, and warmer feelings of love and appreciation than you ever thought possible.

George was feeling out of touch with his wife, Kathy. They both worked and went to school. It seemed they never talked anymore.

Together they looked at both of their schedules. They made Wednesday lunch and Sunday morning brunch dates top priorities. George says now: "I'd never think of missing one of these dates. That is the time we still know we are in tune with each other and share our triumphs and frustrations. We are back to being best friends."

Include Them

Make them feel included in your world, not excluded. Try to create the feeling "We are going to college." If your instructor will allow a visit, and if appropriate, consider taking a family member or friend to a class.

The more they know about what you do, the more they can understand and support you. A Saturday tour around campus can help introduce them to your new world. Take your spouse or older children to athletic events or concerts. Find out if they can use the Physical Education facilities. Bring them to the library with you some evening.

Going back to school can be the best gift you give school-age children. As they study, you study. The message comes through loud and clear; education is a priority here. Gathering together to do your homework can be much more bonding than "zoning out" in front of the TV.

Also, when children know you struggle with school, it gets you off the parental pedestal and on a level leading to better understanding. If your child can help you learn math, so much the better. If they can help demystify the world of computers, you both benefit!

Family and friends need to know they are still a priority in your life. Give them good quality time. Time will be treasured more as the demands of school increase. TV and for fun reading may bite the dust, but good personal relationships are an essential success foundation as you juggle work, home, and school.

Action Review: Checklist of Useful Actions

❏ Have I talked with others about returning to school and how this will affect our lives?

❏ Have I listened well to the concerns of others?

❏ Have I asked for support in a direct, clear, and specific way?

❏ Can I ask for what I need without feeling guilty or demanding?

❏ Do I tell people often enough how much I appreciate their efforts to help?

❏ Do I have a variety of reinforcements available that I can use to express appreciation?

❏ Have I acquainted myself with all the professional resources available to me at school in case I need advice?

❏ Do I have an active, positive plan to make things work out?

Study Buddy Activity

Talk with each other about what you have done to enlist the support of others. Discuss how it feels to make selfish requests. Help each other find ways to handle challenges. Compliment each other for progress you have made. Be sure to tell each other about amusing incidents and your successes.

Chapter 11

How to Balance Going to College with Working

Do you know over 50% of all adult college students work part or full time?

Do you know part-time college students account for the greatest increase in college population?

Do you know most careers will require you to be a life-long learner?

Do you know you can earn college credit by combining work and school?

Scheduling Work and School

Colleges have responded to the needs of students who work. The times and places you take your college classes are becoming more flexible. Evening and weekend courses are available. All-day workshops add options.

If your working hours are flexible you may be able to schedule your courses on Mondays, Wednesdays, and Fridays only, or just mornings or afternoons to accommodate your job. Some companies will arrange a four day work week so you can take three day seminars or attend weekend classes.

Note also that *you do not have to take all of your courses from the same college!* If a course at another college fits your schedule better you may be able to take that course and transfer the credit. Transferring credit is easy to do between state-supported colleges. Be sure and check if the colleges are on a similar school schedule, quarter or semester system.

Course-Load Guidelines

If you work full time, you probably should take no more than two classes in college at one time. The rule of thumb: for every hour of class time, you need two or three hours to do the homework for that class. Thus, if you spend six hours a week in class, you will spend 12 to 18 hours a week in preparation. Add that to a 40-hour work week and you have a sizable commitment. Travel time from work, home and school must also be considered.

If you are going to school full time, work outside school should be kept to 20 or fewer hours. If you work more than 20 hours, work, school, or both are likely to suffer from the overload.

A few students choose jobs that pay less if studying is possible at times on the job. Some students know they need the physical release of a lot of activity after classes and deliberately choose a job involving physical labor.

Work-study jobs can allow split-shift work around class schedules. For some, splitting up school and work is helpful; for others, it is fragmenting. There is no right or wrong way to combine work and school but there is a way that works best for you. The challenge is to find it.

Employers Will Help You

Employers need educated workers. They need people who learn new technology rapidly, work well as a team member, communicate effectively in words and writing, and adapt to a rapidly changing work world.

In recent years employers have created many ways to encourage, support, and pay for the education of the workers they need. It is estimated that industry now spends from $40 to $60 billion on educational training each year. Employers work closely with colleges to offer a variety of ways to blend working with your college education.

Merging Learning and Work

Most colleges now offer programs for getting college credit for work experience. Credit is offered in a variety of ways that include cooperative education, work-study programs, internships, and practicums.

Cooperative Work Experience

Cooperative work experience allows a student to work and earn college credit while exploring a career choice. When a student has chosen a major such as business, computer science, or engineering, the school's cooperative education department can help arrange work experience in the field.

A student may have a particular job site in mind, or the cooperative work specialist may find an appropriate work placement in the student's major field of study. Specific learning experiences are defined and the student is supervised in meeting the objectives. The average co-op student earns $7,000 per year, although some placements are arranged on a volunteer basis.

Cooperative education personnel maintain close contact

with companies designated as co-op sites. Everything is done to ensure a good learning experience.

It is not possible to receive retroactive credit in co-op, but it is possible to earn college credit for present employment. If your present work is within the field of your college major, or you are doing certain kinds of work to see if you wish to make it your major field of study, it is worth contacting your cooperative education department to look into the possibility of receiving college credit for your present job.

Work Study and Student Help

Colleges hire many students to work on campus. The federal government provides funds for the college work-study program. Work-study students must qualify for their jobs by showing financial need.

Student-help jobs are also available. They require only that the student is competent to do the work.

Those in the work-study and student-help programs fill in at libraries, locker rooms, receptionists' desks, laboratories, cafeterias, counseling offices, school grounds, and many other college locations. Usually, they work for the minimum wage but the work experience can be valuable training. It can help clarify career goals and be included on a résumé. These jobs often allow you some study time on the job and your supervisor shifts your work hours to fit your class schedule and exam times.

Everyone Benefits

If you haven't had much paid work experience, a work-study job can be a good confidence builder. It is a way to prove your worth in the work world. The recent trend is for more organizations to offer positions to students. They recognize that involving students in work experience is a good way to screen potential employees. It also helps the work-study student to build job contacts.

Joan, for example, was a single parent struggling to get off welfare. She started working for the counseling department in a clerical capacity as a work-study student. Her work and life experience helped solidify her choice of social work as a college major. The department was able to set up a co-op work experience to help her earn college credits. Later, when Joan needed a practicum site for her degree, the counseling department set up an information referral position in job placement. When she was granted her degree in social work, Joan had incorporated enough practical, professional experience to have a decided edge on other graduates. Valuable contacts and recommendations were hers. Securing a job, using her new credentials, was not difficult.

Internship Programs
An internship is a training position that usually pays you for acquiring a skill. Internships may be offered where expensive equipment or the need for highly trained professionals make on-the-job training cost effective. Prerequisite skills are taught in the classroom, but most of the new learning takes place in the work place.

Two vocational career fields that use internships extensively are electronic engineering technician and radio/TV broadcasting. These industries grow and change so rapidly that few colleges have the funds or facilities for the latest equipment. Neither can the colleges meet salary scales to hire top people in these fields.

A partnership is formed where education experts break the learning process into manageable steps, write the curriculum, assign credit, provide on-site consultation, and see that complementary classwork is provided. Internship programs often lead to a two-year associate degree, or may be a requirement for an advanced degree.

Practicum Training Experiences
Practicum experiences differ from internships in that they often require a year or more of classroom work before a student is allowed on-the-job practical experience. Paraprofessional programs (teacher assistant, legal assistant, alcohol/drug counselor) have significant practical experience as an essential part of their vocational degree program.

On-the-job training may take anywhere from three months to more than a year. This practicum training is coupled with classroom discussion and job supervision. (Note: students *rarely* receive payment for practicum experience. The personal supervision you receive from experts is valuable compensation.)

Balancing Predictable School and Work Demands

Many jobs have peak demand periods. In school, it's mid-terms and finals. In retail sales, pre-Christmas shopping will keep you hopping. For colleges, fall registration is a busy time for support services. If you have school-age children summer vacation can be extra demanding.

When work times are predictably busy, lighten your school load to accommodate busy times. Get that paper in early; move ahead in your reading; talk with your teacher to get a jump on early work—or an approved delay, if needed.

For those who juggle work and school, knowing about and using your options are survival tools. Trying to cram full-time work, full-time school, and demanding personal relationships into twenty-four hours can lead a person to early burnout. It is not how fast you can get there, but rather, are you enjoying the process? Can you go the distance? That's what counts!

Bread and Butter Jobs (that don't interfere with academic success)

If you need a "bread and butter" job to help with expenses while you go to school, don't expect it to be the delight of your dreams. You can, however, make it work with your school schedule. It would be a bonus if it were somehow related to your career choice, but it does not have to be connected. What is essential is that you can earn a certain amount of money to take care of the "bread and butter" of survival.

How do you find such a job? The same rules apply here that you use searching for career employment. In a nutshell:

- Know what skills and personal qualities you have to offer.
- Let everyone know you are looking for a job.

- Be prepared to state your case with enthusiasm.
- Practice common job interview questions and answers.
- Make contacts at best hours and days, Tuesday-Thursday, 10 a.m.-11 a.m. and 2 p.m.-3 p.m.
- Dress for success, be clean, careful, conservative, classic.
- Let your attitude show you really want the job.
- You "make it or break it" in the first three minutes of the interview.
- Keep employer's needs in mind.
- Have accurate information ready for job application.
- Tell them the best time of day to contact you and what phone number to call.
- Send a thank-you note for the interview.
- Before accepting a job consider the location. Is it close to campus or will commuting be a problem?
- Be alert to opportunities. A "bread and butter" job can lead to a "caviar and champagne" career!

Hopefully, this information has expanded your thinking about what is available for college students in the way of employment these days. Look around. Talk with people. It may be that you can find a work situation that fits your schedule and your educational program while providing you with much needed income.

College, Work, Family, Friends, and Time For You

The guidelines and suggestions in chapters 11 and 12 are being used successfully by many students. It is possible to combine going to college with studying, family life, a job, and still have time for yourself too. Here is what one student reported:

> I had no ideas how many hours of studying were necessary for class. I found myself adding up the hours in a week and realized something would have to give. I sat down and developed my "Study Schedule," my "Me-Time Schedule," my "Family Schedule," and finally, my "Work Schedule." Now my time is allocated so that I can make the best use of it.

Many students find that when they organize their time better, ask others for help or understanding, and work only on the most important things to be done, they can accomplish much more than they ever thought possible. As we've said before, you don't have to be an extraordinary person to succeed in college. All you have to do is be in control of what you do with yourself.

Action Review

Check the following list for balancing work and school:

❏ Do I make realistic school and work demands on myself?

❏ Have I explored the possibility of getting college credit for work experience?

❏ Have I asked my employer about ways that my educational efforts could be paid for or reimbursed?

❏ Have I looked at new developments and changes in the job market?

❏ Have I combined employment with career development opportunities?

Study Buddy Activity

Do the members of your group work? What sort of balance between work and study have you each arranged? What do you know about ways to work for pay, earn college credit, and gain on-the-job experience? Does someone in your group have some job information you can use?

Chapter 12

Celebrating Diversity

Are you aware some of your best education is getting to know and appreciate people from other cultures?

Do you realize that a person's cultural background starts imprinting in earliest childhood?

Are you aware there are more women in college today than men?

Do you know the work world is giving added importance to employees knowing more than one language?

The College Environment Is Like the Work World

Today's workplace requires skills at understanding and working with people from different ethnic and cultural backgrounds. The dynamics involved in personal interactions in college are similar to those found in the work world.

College is not just a place to get new information. It is a place where exchanging views, learning about different life styles, getting new perspectives, and gaining insights can open up paths that lead to a more satisfying life. The college setting is a safe place where the pay check is not threatened when you discuss, argue, exchange views, adapt to other's differences, try new things, and meet new people. This is why some of your most important learning in college is of an interpersonal nature, not just an academic one.

Demographics And Attitudes Are Changing

The United States has been known as a "melting pot" for different cultures and ethnic groups. An attitude that existed among many was, "Learn our language, customs, and values. If you can not fit in here, go somewhere else."

We are a very young country, and maybe could be excused for some of our tunnel vision in the past. Social awareness and current events, however, show that "melting pot" idealism has not worked very well. Social unrest along with a rapid increase in minority populations has shifted attitudes toward the necessity of respecting and understanding differences in people's languages, cultural heritage, family roots, customs, and values.

Native Americans lived in this land for thousands of years, respecting the trees, waters, land and sky. They did not believe in individual ownership of these resources, but believed they belonged to all. Their respect for nature, often dismissed by whites, is now known to be critical to the survival of our environment. Preserving the resources of this earth are now seen as an essential value by many.

African Americans were brought to this country with the shackles of slavery curbing their freedom. They bonded together forming strong ties to family and churches to gain comfort and find ways to survive in a hostile society. The strength of these ties is now recognized and seen as a model for others to copy.

People of Hispanic background come in ever increasing numbers to the United States, hoping for a better life. The richness of their language and culture is serving as incentive for many people to become bilingual.

Asian immigrants bring a wealth of languages and a strong work ethic to this country. To build a future for their families they often combine full time school and full time work. This reminds us of the hard work and pioneering spirit that built this country.

Older students, with the variety of work and life experience, bring the perspective of generations to understanding current events as well as course content.

The Gift of a Broader View
Prejudice handicaps learning. People from different backgrounds, religions, and cultures provide a perspective to life, work and education that allows a richer learning environment. To ignore this source of added value to your education would be to deprive yourself of one of your greatest opportunities. There are many academic, social, political, and career decisions ahead of you. Developing empathy and understanding for the views, values, and visions of others is a survival skill as well as a gift of personal enrichment.

Changing Faces in Our Cities
In American cities the population mix is shifting rapidly. At present, in New York City about 20% of the population is African American, 20% are foreign born. In Dallas-Fort Worth about 15% are African American, 20% foreign born, and 15% are Hispanic. In San Francisco-Oakland-San Jose about 10% are African American, 20% are foreign born, and 18% are Hispanic. The Hispanic population is our fastest growing minority group. According to projections, in a few decades white Euro-Americans will be less than 50% of the U.S. population.

College Campuses Reflect the Cultural Shift

On college campuses white Euro-Americans now make up less than 80% of the college population. At the University of California at Berkeley, white Euro-Americans are less than 50% of the students enrolled.

Almost 55% of the students in college are women. The traditionally male universities such as Harvard, Yale, and Princeton are now seeking a gender balance and are actively recruiting women students. The same is true of women's colleges as many of them recruit men to their campuses. One result of this is that the male dominated professions such as law, engineering, and medicine are seeing great increases in women students.

Students who are over twenty-five, are seen in greater numbers at campuses all over the United States. Smaller families, decreased family obligations, changing work world, financial pressure and/or ability, and intellectual curiosity all contribute to this changing scene.

We each come to college with cultural, social, economic, and political backgrounds that we started absorbing in our early childhood. What games did we play? Were we raised in a small family or in a large family with friends and relatives also important in our upbringing?

Was education looked on as an important value? Which was more important, taking care of your self or taking care of your family? How do your present ideas and values differ from the family you were raised in? If some values differ, was the changing easy or difficult?

Were you encouraged to learn a second language by your family? Discouraged from doing so?

IIII➤ In the years ahead being bilingual will greatly increase your chances for employment and career success.

The Price May Be High But the Benefit is Bigger

Comparing your personal history to others, whether in the family, your neighborhood, your work, or at school can be challenging, frustrating, and rewarding. Differences in the way things are viewed and handled can lead to conflict. Change does not come about easily. On a personal level, you have to decide how much you wish to increase your tolerance and comfort level with people much different than you.

A major barrier to decreasing prejudice is found in the attitudes of close friends and family. If you made friends with someone from a different race or background, how would your friends and family react if they found out? Are your friendships determined by what is acceptable to others? It can be a dilemma.

Keep in mind also that learning to fit into society so that you can be successful does not mean giving up your culture or values. Indian students, for example, find that going to pow wows and maintaining connections with their elders and spiritual leaders gives them strength and stability that many white students lack. Finding the right balance for you is a "do-it-yourself" job.

If your background or present situation makes you feel different and conflict and confusion arises, it can be helpful to talk about the struggle with family members, friends, and counselors. The struggle can be great but the rewards can be greater. It will prepare you for the world of tomorrow in which you will become an active participant in making a better life for yourself and others.

Different Backgrounds Can Create Difficulties

Your culture may tell you to listen quietly and respectfully to those in authority and not to question their views. Yet, the professor urges you to participate by asking questions and challenging his ideas.

You may have been raised to think that as a female you are not to meet a male's eyes. Yet, the instructor interprets the lack of eye contact as a sign of disinterest.

Your sense of time may be more in tune with showing an appreciation of seasonal changes than with the discipline of studying the week before finals. This could bring you a lower grade in a class weighted heavily toward tests.

You may have been raised to be very verbal and express your feelings with passion, but now you receive negative comments for your long emotional statements in class.

Your instructor is impressed with your skill in math and science and encourages you to make engineering your major, but being female you know your family will only encourage your brothers to earn professional degrees. You are to be a clerical worker.

Your instructor comes highly recommended for her knowledge in your field of study, but you can not understand her because of a heavy accent.

These are all examples of how culture background, yours or someone else's, plays a role in your decisions as a student. These cultural differences also affect your personal relations.

On The Homefront, Roles Are Re-examined

No one in your family has ever gone to college before. Your family does not understand the many hours of study you must do when you get home. They think you are drawing away from them and have become less important to you. You see time spent studying as the best way to help your family.

You have always been interested in how things work and the idea of studying auto mechanics appeals to you but your family says you will study accounting. American students seem to make choices just for themselves, not for the good of their families. Should individual choice be more important than family choice? Values are different here. Change brings conflict yet affords the opportunity to grow and reexamine.

Personal Touch versus Institutional Distance

If you like to have lots of friends, like to know many people by name and have many others knowing you by name, the apparent coldness of a large institution with many rules and regulations can feel very uncomfortable. You may feel like a walking social security number, rather than your real self.

Has your background emphasized formal manners, where the hierarchy of authority is clearly defined and respected? If so, it may be hard to relate to the casual, informal, egalitarian approach of American students who insist on their personal rights regardless of group needs.

The straight lecture method where the student takes notes may be what you are used to. If so, you may now feel confused by the discussion, interaction, and questioning that is expected of you in some of your classes. All of this requires adjustment on your part and may test your patience.

Many Advantages

Instead of retaining a view of the U.S. as a "melting pot," the image of a "stir fry" may be more appropriate. In a stir fry each ingredient is separate, but adds to the flavor and distinction of the entire dish. It is time to breath new life into our personal and national recipe, to change the metaphor to allow a more international flavor.

Class discussions, study buddy groups, campus social activities, student government, meal times in the cafeteria, and the college newspaper all afford opportunity for exchanging social, philosophical, political, and personal views. Students from different ethnic and cultural backgrounds have special conferences and celebrations open for everyone to attend.

It is in this way we can gain the intellectual and personal insights which allow us to take an educated and humane place in our world culture. We are all teachers and we are all learners!

Action Review

❏ Have I examined how cultural influences affect my reactions to others and the choices I make?

❏ Am I aware of how different cultural views affect people's work and life styles?

❏ Do I see the benefits to be gained from increased awareness of other cultures?

❏ Have I made efforts to know, appreciate, and respect people from other cultures?

❏ Have I attended meetings or gatherings put on by students from other cultures at my college?

Study Buddy Activities

Have each person in your group prepare a personal cultural profile. Include social, political, economic, and religious attitudes in your family of origin. Set up a time when you have lunch with at least two students of significantly different backgrounds. Discuss differences and similarities in your cultural profiles. With your study group examine what you learned that was new. What surprised you? What did you have in common?

Are any of you bilingual? Talk about how being bilingual would affect your lives.

Surviving
and
Thriving
in a
Changing World

Chapter 13

How to Handle Pressure Well

Do you know the difference between stress and strain?

Do you believe the way for your life to get better is for other people to change?

Did you know stress can be good for you?

Can you be both optimistic and pessimistic?

Do you know how to decrease your negative experiences and increase your positive experiences?

How to Handle Pressure and Strain

Some people deal with pressure better than others. You probably have several friends or acquaintances who are very durable and resilient. They cope well with life's difficulties. You probably also know several people who almost fall apart going through an ordinary day.

This chapter will show how to hold up well under the many pressures that can build up when you have to attend classes and study while you handle other important responsibilities, work, and raise a family. Before we look at practical ways to increase your resiliency, however, we need to clarify some misunderstandings about stress.

Stress has received a bad name in recent years. Many people think stress is bad. It isn't. *Too much* stress may be bad for you, a certain amount is necessary for health and well-being.

1. Selye made a mistake.

Much of the confusion and misunderstanding about stress traces back to Dr. Hans Selye, the physician who created the concept *biological stress* in 1936. In his memoirs, however, he apologized for using the wrong term. He explained that when he came from Europe to attend medical school he did not understand either the English language or physics very well. He said his research was about strain, not stress. He said he should have named his concept the *strain syndrome*.

2. There is no stress in any situation until a person experiences strain.

In physics a stressor is an external force attempting to deform an object. The affect on an object is measured as strain. Human beings differ so widely in their abilities to handle various situations, what is mildly challenging for one person is overwhelming for another.

3. Many people blame the situation for their reaction to it.

It is not unusual to hear people claim that they have stressful jobs, stresses at home, or stresses as college students. That is a misperception. They are confusing the situation with their reaction to it. It isn't the circumstance that counts, it is your reaction to it that counts. What is distressing for one person is an easy workout for another. An instructor that one student complains about for being extremely tough is appreciated by another for setting high standards.

4. Stressful situations can be beneficial.

Selye coined the term *eustress* to emphasize that everyone needs a certain level of stress. When we work at handling the strains we engage, we gradually get stronger. Athletes build up their physical strength with frequent workouts. Professional training programs build competence by straining people to their limits. Emotionally stressful experiences can motivate people to learn new coping skills. Some mothers, for example, handle the addition of a fourth child to the family more easily than they handled having their first child.

Stress Resistant Personalities

Two people in an identical situation will have different reactions to it. Erma Bombeck wrote many books about her amusing experiences raising a family. Other mothers are so distressed trying to raise their families they need tranquilizers, counseling, and emotional support.

The situation a person is in is not the problem. *It is how a person deals with a situation* that explains why some people become sick while others become strong in the same environment. The following list summarizes the research findings about persons less likely to develop stress related illness. As you read the list check to see how well it describes you:

__ few upsetting events in routine activities;

__ feel capable of taking effective action about upsetting events;

__ draw action choices from a wide range of inner and external resources;

__ experience family and friends as caring and supportive;

___ manage self-change well; and

___ convert negative experiences into beneficial learning.

Recognize the Signs of Not Coping Well

Indicators that the pressures are getting to be too much include: sleepless nights, drinking alcohol to get to sleep, losing your temper over a minor incident, migraine headaches, frequent colds and illnesses, auto accidents, ulcers flaring up, high blood pressure and other cardiovascular problems, losing track of time, falling asleep in class, and forgetting to bring a paper you stayed up late at night to finish.

How to Cope Effectively With Lots of Pressures

For most adult students, the challenge is not having to deal with one major difficulty, the challenge is how to hold up week after week handling a whole lot of little things.

It is important to avoid feeling helpless and at the mercy of external forces. Here is a practical plan of action for decreasing emotional strain while increasing your hardiness and resiliency.

Decrease the pressures.

1. *Make a list of everything you experience as negative, upsetting, or stressful.*

   Sometimes the only way to be more positive is let yourself be negative. When you make a list of everything you feel pressured about, you are not a negative person, you are an emotionally healthy person taking the first step toward coping well. Listing all the forces working against you is the first step for preparing to deal with them.

2. *Express your feelings about your list.*

   It is not unusual to experience some physical and emotional upsets when you start college for the first time. Forgetfulness, stomach and intestinal problems, and sleeping difficulties are normal reactions to stress. These symptoms are usually temporary and should diminish quickly if you find outlets for your feelings.

3. *Go through your list, item by item, asking questions:*
   - Could I do something about this? How direct is my contact?
   - What if I ignored this or avoided contact?
   - Could I change the situation in some way? Who could help me?
   - What if I changed my reaction to it?

The aim is to find ways to minimize the impact of the entire list. It isn't usually one big thing that does a person in, it is the accumulation of many little things. With this plan you diminish the effects of too many strains, avoid feeling helpless, and increase feelings of emotional control.

> Although I'm a pretty relaxed person most of the time, I did learn to recognize when stress was building up. I finally figured out that from time to time I would develop this overwhelming urge to clean the house, which meant that I was feeling too much pressure. I knew that things were really bad when the urge to clean the house changed and became specific—*I wanted to clean the refrigerator!*—MK

Increase positive and revitalizing experiences.

1. *Make a list of things you experience as positive in your life.*
   Ask yourself what activities make you feel happy and relaxed. What makes you feel good? Reflect on pleasant experiences.

2. *Ask questions about how to repeat, increase, or have new positive experiences.*
   - Am I ignoring or taking for granted some positive aspects?
   - What do I enjoy doing? What do I get enthusiastic about?
   - What would I like to do that I keep putting off?
   - With whom do I enjoy sharing good experiences?

3. *Do several things good for you to do.*
   It is important to be self-nourishing even though it may look

like selfishness. Psychologically healthy people are both un-selfish and selfish. They act in ways that are good for their well-being while still being helpful to others.

Develop Healthy Self-Esteem

Your self-esteem influences how well you do in college and in life. Many people were trained by their parents to never brag, be stuck up, or conceited. As a result, many people have never developed a healthy level of self-esteem. It takes courage to defy old parental prohibitions, but it must be done to achieve and enjoy success.

Without strong self-esteem you will probably find it diffi-cult to even imagine getting a high grade point average. Your expectations and actions are controlled by worries about what others might think. You are afraid that if you got top grades others would think that you think you are superior to them.

Self-esteem is your opinion of yourself. Strong self-esteem is like a thick emotional skin. It acts as a buffer to shrug off hurtful criticisms. When someone is critical, your self-esteem lets you decide that you like your opinion of yourself better than theirs. Self-esteem lets you appreciate compliments. It de-termines how much you learn after something goes wrong.

Self-esteem is strengthened by positive self-talk. Make a list of all the things you like and appreciate about yourself.

Overcoming the "Good Child" Handicap

The plan outlined here will decrease feelings of pressure, in-crease revitalizing experiences, and increase your ability to do well in your courses. It is simple, effective plan that will in-crease your hardiness and resiliency.

If you were raised to be a "good girl" or a "good boy" this coping plan will be difficult. You were raised to never be nega-tive, never act in selfish ways, and never be prideful or stuck-up. Your parents had good intentions, but trying to go through life acting like a good five year old is a handicap in a constantly changing world.

Mentally healthy people can list what they are unhappy about, make requests of others, and include themselves on their list of people they do nice things for. Here are some things to consider doing for yourself:

Revitalizing Activities

Laugh and Play With Friends
Successful students do not study all the time. Do anything you can to prevent your college life from getting too serious, too burdensome, and too heavy. Make a conscious effort to get into activities where you can laugh or play hard and completely forget your responsibilities at school and home.

Stay Physically Active
Do anything each week that works your muscles. This might be bike riding, gardening, jogging, playing racquetball or tennis, swimming, or fast walking. It may be a yoga class. In any case, activities that work your muscles increase your physical tiredness and help you sleep and rest better. If you are not doing much of this now, take another look at the recreation facilities on campus.

Take Naps, Meditate, or Listen to Music
Naps are a wonderful way to relax and revitalize yourself. If you have a car at school, try taking naps in your car. Take a short nap early in the evening instead of watching television before studying. Take naps on weekends if you wish.

Research into meditation shows that it has many beneficial effects. Find a place where you can sit and do nothing for a few minutes each day. Don't use the time to solve problems. Focus your attention on a beautiful scene. Recall one of your most enjoyable vacations. Take easy, relaxing breaths. Most counseling centers have useful books and cassette tapes on how to increase relaxation and reduce stress.

An option is to sit and listen to classical music while doing nothing else. Sit back and totally lose yourself in the music. The word "music" means something that enhances musing. So do it. Muse.

Drawbacks of Unexpressed Emotions

Sometimes school, work, and family pressures are not the problem. Did you lose your job through no fault of your own? Were you laid off in a very insensitive way? Have you been through a divorce that now makes your life more difficult than you ever expected?

Have you dealt with your emotions about these disrupting events? It is important to consciously uncover and acknowledge your feelings because *if you haven't resolved your angry feelings, you will not be able to study, not become involved with your new life direction, and you will be less effective in employment interviews.*

Strong unresolved feelings have more power over you than feelings you have expressed and "processed." People who don't allow themselves to feel and express strong emotions often experience flare-ups of anger, distrust, hostility, or despair.

The Benefits of Purging Upsetting Emotions

If you find yourself sitting in class and haven't heard anything the instructor said for ten minutes because you've been holding an internal emotional conversation with the people who disrupted your life, you need to do something.

Psychologist James Pennebaker has developed a very helpful technique to use. He was asked, for example, to help a group of professional people who had been laid off and were unable to find work. He put them in a conference room and had them write about their deepest thoughts and feelings surrounding the layoff and how their lives had been affected. They wrote as fast as they could without regard for spelling or neatness. They did this for about twenty minutes a day five days in a row.

Three months later 23% of the group had full-time employment. Eight months later 53% had full-time employment, several more had satisfactory part-time employment, and one had started his own business. When interviewed, they all said they found the experience of writing about their feelings so helpful *they wished they had been made to do it much sooner!*

Mentally healthy people express angry feelings and grieve their losses as part of their transition to a new life. If you haven't dealt with upsetting losses, start writing about your feelings.

The Counseling Center Can Help

Most college students have periods of feeling lonely and depressed. If this happens to you, remember that such feelings are part of being human. School counselors can show you how to get through an unpleasant period while the natural emotional processes of self-healing are operating.

Emotional upsets are normal. You don't have to handle them alone. It is not a sign of strength to mask your feelings with drugs or put on a front of happiness. Emotional strength develops from feeling whatever you feel and talking to friends when things aren't working well. Get some help from your friends, family, and other resources when things aren't so great.

Getting Stronger and Stronger

- The ability to handle many pressures over a long period of time can be learned. An effective plan of action includes reducing negative, stressful experiences while increasing positive, revitalizing experiences.
- By seeing that a stressful experience is a feeling of strain that you don't like, you avoid feeling victimized. You can use strain like a workout. Just as bike riding, jogging, or swimming leads to getting physically stronger, using emotional strains as workouts leads to becoming mentally and emotionally stronger.
- It isn't the situation that matters, it is your reaction to it that counts. Martha Washington once observed:

  I am still determined to be cheerful and happy in whatever situation I may be, for I have also learned from experience that the greater part of our happiness or misery depends upon our dispositions and not upon our circumstances.

- What is distressing for one person is not stressful for another. When you take steps to cope with pressures and negative experiences, you will experience less stress and strain.

Action Review

☐ I have listed all the things I experience as negative, and developed plans for reducing, changing, avoiding, or minimizing them.

☐ I have listed what is positive and revitalizing for me and have a plan for increasing my pleasant, revitalizing experiences.

☐ I am able to consciously like and appreciate myself.

☐ I understand the feeling of distress is emotional strain and that strain can lead to getting stronger and better.

Study Buddy Activity

Talk about the pressures you each feel. Ask each other "How do you manage?" Find out what you each do that is enjoyable, positive, and revitalizing.

Discuss your reactions to reading that an important step toward thriving under pressure is to list everything you feel negative about. Was it difficult to express negative feelings?

Talk about how you might have been raised to be a "good child" who never complains, is not selfish, and has low self-esteem.

Discuss how easy or difficult it is to engage in activities that may seem selfish. How have others reacted when you've acted in selfish ways? Discuss your feelings about developing strong self-esteem.

Did a disruptive change such as job loss or divorce lead to your enrolling in college? If so, how well have you dealt with your feelings about this matter?

Chapter 14

Thriving in a World of Constant Change

Do you understand how curiosity, playfulness, intuition, and humor are related to thriving?

Do you know how to learn useful lessons from everyday experiences?

Do you know it is healthy to be paradoxical?

Do you know the value of developing an attitude of professionalism?

The World is Changing, Are You?

People who thrive in a constantly changing world are different from people who fit into an unchanging world.

For many decades, children have been trained by parents and teachers to act, dress, talk, feel, and think as told. This training produced millions of high school graduates conditioned to be obedient employees in large organizations that changed very slowly. If you were an obedient employee who followed your job description, were receptive to performance evaluations, and didn't cause problems for managers, you could expect to eventually be old enough to stay home and still get checks.

In recent years, however, the speed of change has accelerated. Large organizations, to become leaner and more agile, laid off tens of thousands of managers and workers. Employees who thought they were set for life found themselves out of work. The employees who kept their jobs usually found that they had to work harder and longer just to keep their jobs a few months more.

What is Your Response to Disruptive Change?

How do you react to life's difficulties? Do you have a victim/blaming reaction or a surviving/thriving reaction?

The victim reaction is to be crushed by the blow. The victim habit is to complain: "This isn't fair!" "They've ruined my life." "Look what they've done to me." And "I won't be able to find another job." People with victim patterns feel helpless. They blame others for their unhappy circumstances.

The person who survives and thrives during disruptive change is much different than the obedient employee of the past. Life's best survivors have a learning/coping reaction when unfairly hit with an unexpected disruption. When hurt and distressed they expect to find a way to have things turn out well. They react to adversities by learning lessons in the school of life and they develop new strengths.

People who thrive in constant change are agile, flexible, adapt quickly, synergistic, learn from experience, gain strength from adversity, and have a talent for serendipity. They handle major difficulties better than most people. When hit by major setbacks they don't complain about life being unfair.

Journalist Terry Anderson, for example, was taken hostage in Lebanon and held for almost seven years. He was beaten, fed poorly, and ordered to not talk with other hostages. Did he become angry and bitter? No. During the press conference held after his release he was cheerful and in good humor about his ordeal. He described how he coped and how he developed a sign language that let him communicate with other hostages. He said the years he spent in captivity "weren't wasted." His older sister said she could see that he was different and better than he was before.

Life's best survivors get better and better with age. Like cats, they manage to land on their feet when the bottom drops out of their lives.

Professionalism is Replacing Job Descriptions

People who thrive in constant change do not need detailed job descriptions. They have a strong attitude of professionalism that lets them find ways to be useful and successful in new and ambiguous situations.

Changes in the workplace now occur so rapidly it is rare for anyone to have an up-to-date job description. Some corporations have stopped giving people job descriptions. They have job categories for determining compensation levels, but they now rely on people who know how to make themselves useful, work well with others, and are constantly adapting and learning. Employers are searching for people with professionalism.

How to Increase Your Thriving Strengths and Your Professionalism

Years of research shows that there is a strong similarity between a person with professionalism and a person who gains strength from life's difficult experiences. A person with the following qualities and personality traits is most likely to succeed and thrive in a rapidly changing, sometimes unfair world.

Create Good Synergy: Focus on Making Things Work Well

People who thrive in times of change are those who need and expect difficult situations to eventually work out all right. They create a good "flow" in their part of the world. They get maximum results with minimum time and energy. The way they interact with people and situations has a synergistic effect. That is why they are good people to have around. They have a knack for knowing what to focus on and what to ignore, what to stick with and what to change.

Needing to have things work well makes a person comfortable with constant change. Having things to work better requires giving up or changing old practices, assumptions, and beliefs. When a better way of doing things comes along, people with professionalism adopt them easily.

This need for good synergy is the internal, organizing frame of reference for thriving in ambiguous, new, changing, situations. When faced with a disruptive situation a person avoids reacting like a victim by thinking "How can I interact with this so that things work out well for everyone?"

Child-Like Curiosity is a Survival Skill

To handle change or a disruptive situation well, you must read the new reality rapidly. You must quickly and accurately understand and comprehend what is happening.

Being open to read, assess, and respond to new developments is a reflex in people who adapt faster and better than others. It is a brain habit based on retaining a childlike curiosity throughout one's life.

Do you ask lots of questions? Wonder how things work? Wonder how and why other people do what they do?

This sort of curiosity gives a person a mind that quickly comprehends upsetting developments and changes that bewilder others. People who thrive in a changing world are accustomed to what is unusual, complicated, and mysterious. That is why, when hit with disruptive change and unexpected difficulties, they quickly absorb information about what is happening.

Playful Humor Makes a Big Difference

Threats and crises can trigger a person's inborn "fight or flight" response. A strong surge of adrenaline can increase the speed of your muscular reflexes and your muscle strength, but it impairs good problem solving. That is why laughing or joking during a crisis is very practical!

Why does humor help? Laughing reduces tension. Creative problem solving, accurate thinking, and good physical coordination are best in moderate emotional states. Alan Alda's irreverent humor as Hawkeye in the television series "M.A.S.H." was an excellent example. He was serious about being a surgeon but not about being a soldier. Hawkeye's sense of humor is typical of people who are best at dealing with emergencies and dicey situations.

The humor is not hostile or hurtful. It is directed toward the situation. The person toys with what is happening and pokes fun at it. Chances for surviving are increased by the attitude, "I am bigger than this situation. This is my toy. I am going to play with it."

Humorous playing is a way of asking "How does this look from a different point of view? What would happen if I turned it upside down? What if the reverse were true? What unusual things exist here?" By playing and toying with the situation, the person avoids being overwhelmed and at the same time is likely to come up with a way to survive.

How about you? Have you ever been poked in the ribs for muttering a humorous comment during a serious moment? If so, that is a good sign.

Be Adaptable and Flexible

Survivors of extreme adversity say that the most important quality in survival is to be flexible and adaptable. A person must be able to do something different than they ever did before, perhaps even the opposite.

What makes inner flexibility possible? Counter-balanced personality traits. They let you be both one way *and* the opposite, both pessimistic and optimistic, for example.

Can a person be both? Yes. Life's best survivors are comfortable with their paradoxical qualities even though the popular thinking is that people are either one way or the other, such as either pessimistic *or* optimistic.

Paradoxical or counter-balanced personality traits are something like having both extensor and flexor muscles in your arm. You can make your arms, hands, and fingers do what you want because you control the choice point between two sets of opposing muscles.

How flexible and paradoxical are you? Look at the two lists. Check off the traits you possess. Add traits not listed in the spaces at the bottom.

❏ calm	❏ emotional
❏ trusting	❏ cautious
❏ strong	❏ gentle
❏ serious	❏ playful
❏ lazy	❏ hard-working
❏ stingy	❏ generous
❏ curious	❏ indifferent
❏ self-confident	❏ self-critical
❏ pessimistic	❏ optimistic
❏ unselfish	❏ selfish
❏ _____	❏ _____
❏ _____	❏ _____

If you looked at the lists and quickly decided "All of the above, depending on the situation," that's wonderful. If you wrote down several more pairs of paradoxical or contradictory qualities you've noticed about yourself, that is an *excellent* sign.

It is important to understand that the lists are not meant to be a comprehensive listing of all possible pairs. The two lists are there to demonstrate an important point. Being paradoxical gives you flexibility and the more pairs of paradoxical traits you have, the more flexible you are at dealing with any situation that develops. If you identify with having many such contradictory traits you will have many more pairs than those listed.

Having opposing personality traits is like having a reverse gear in a car. It lets you back up when you need to. People without many counter-balanced or paradoxical pairs of traits are emotionally handicapped. They are rigid and inflexible because they were trained to be one-sided. They were taught to never be selfish, angry, negative, lazy, or self-appreciating.

One-sided people are difficult to live and work with. They have an energy draining effect on work teams. They are so concerned about acting as they think they should, they interfere with things working well.

It is also true that some people have so many contrary qualities they are flaky. They have an energy draining effect on work teams because they are emotionally scattered and disorganized. The professional person has found a way to exercise easy control over how and when to jump the tracks.

Both Creative and Traditional
Creativity is the ability to come up with a new way of doing things that works. The creativity essential for agility and thriving derives from the need to have things work well and having a paradoxical nature. The need to have things work well gives a person an inner frame of reference for choosing between doing something unusual or staying with what is working quite well. This is why people with highly developed professionalism are both creative and traditional in the way they work.

Practice Intuition and Empathy
The people who thrive in a variety of situations trust their intuition and have good empathy skills. They monitor their own internal emotional state and can read the emotional states of others as well.

Coping with new situations often depends on a sense that

something is wrong. A tight stomach or an uneasy feeling may be the clue. These feelings can be set off by anything—a person's tone of voice, something not said, a group's quietness, anything at all that doesn't fit.

Women are usually better than men at using intuition because most women are raised practicing it. Men who practice intuition can develop the same ability, however, because it is based on subliminal perception—something that exists within every human.

People who handle others well are able to step out of their own feelings and views to empathize with the feelings and perceptions of others. As you will see in the next chapter, people most likely to be successful in job interviews start by conducting interviews about the organization they would like to look for. A company won't hire you because you need money to pay your bills. They may hire you if you can present yourself as having skills they need.

Empathy does *not* mean you are a weak, easily hurt bleeding heart. Survivor empathy is the kind Abraham Lincoln used during his years as a defense attorney. He was very successful because he would begin his opening statements to the jury presenting a better case against his client than the opposing attorney was prepared to do.

Here is an example of how empathy led an electronics specialist to remain working for a corporation even though his job was eliminated through downsizing. One morning he was informed by his manager that his position was being eliminated. The specialist knew his work was critical for completing an important new product. He looked at the situation from the perspective of the managers and executives. He saw that they need someone with his skills. He inquired about how the company would get essential work done without employees qualified to do it. He learned that consultants would be hired.

He wrote up his qualifications to be a consultant to the company and made an appointment with the project engineer. He explained how critical his skills were. The engineer agreed and arranged to hire him as a consultant. The man says he remained at his same work station and kept on doing the same work.

Empathy includes understanding people who live and think in disliked ways, including the manager who may have laid you off. The attitude of the empathy described here is "whether I like you or dislike you, I am going to understand you as well as you understand yourself—and maybe better."

Change Requires Learning

If you look in an introductory psychology textbook you will find that "Learning" will usually be defined as "A relatively permanent change in behavior that results from experience."

Do you see the point? Change and learning go together. You can't have one without the other. Learning leads to change; change requires learning.

When faced with life or job changes that no parent or teacher prepared you for, you must manage your learning by asking questions and finding your own answers. To react to life as a school means to ask questions such as:

Why did they do that? What do they believe will be accomplished? What do I need to do differently now? How are certain important things going to get done?

Professional people and people who thrive learn valuable lessons from bad experiences. Here are the steps to follow:

1. Ask "What happened?"
2. Replay the incident as an observer.
3. Describe what happened. Put it into words.
4. Ask "What can I learn from this? What is the lesson here?"
5. Ask "Next time, what will I do differently?"
6. The next time a person says that to me, what will I say?
7. Imagine yourself handling the situation well the next time.
8. See and feel yourself getting the outcome you desire.
9. Rehearse the effective response.

When you follow these steps for self-managed learning, you will increase your self-confidence and look forward to the next incident with positive anticipation. In contrast, a person who dwells on a past experience with anger and distress anticipates the next incident with dread and does not expect a good outcome. This is why whatever you expect to happen, whether good or bad, usually determines the way things turn out.

Keep Learning in the School of Life

Abraham Maslow is quoted as saying that no one achieves full self-actualization until the age of sixty. He saw that people who constantly learn from experience get better and better decade after decade.

Your most valuable learning comes from the school of life. Throughout this book, whenever we addressed a difficult situation, our approach has been to show you that no matter what happens, you have the inborn ability to handle the difficulty in a way that makes you a stronger, more capable person.

Find a Way to Convert Misfortune into Good Fortune

You may have heard the word *serendipity*. Horace Walpole coined the term to describe a person having the *wisdom* to see that an *accident* or unfortunate development is actually a stroke of *good fortune*.

Your talent for serendipity comes from asking questions such as "Why is it good that this happened?" "What is the gift this brings me?" "What problem does this solve?"

Perhaps you have heard someone say that losing their job, getting cancer, or being divorced was one of the best things that ever happened to them. Can you look back at a rough situation and appreciate that it was also good for you?

We humans have the ability to find value in bad experiences and convert misfortune into good luck. The better you are at thriving and practicing professionalism, the more you will avoid reacting to disruptive change like a victim and can find the joy of serendipity in rough situations.

Action Review: Professionalism and Thriving Skills

❏ When disruptive change is forced on me do I react by coping and learning?

❏ Would former co-workers describe me as having an attitude of professionalism?

❏ Am I good at making things work well?

❏ Do I feel comfortable being paradoxical?

❏ Am I known to be a playful, curious person?

❏ Can I count on my hunches and intuition?

❏ Do I have good empathy skills?

❏ Do I learn good lessons from daily experiences?

❏ Am I able to turn misfortune into good luck?

❏ Have I discovered that one of the worst experiences in my life was also one of the best things that ever happened?

Study Buddy Activity

Describe from your own experience the difference between people who thrive well in difficult situations and people who can turn an ordinary day into a horrible experience.

Describe the difference between people who bring an attitude of professionalism to their work and people who are qualified, but have an unprofessional attitude.

Talk with each other about your reaction to learning it is desirable to have paradoxical personality traits. Were you raised to be one way but not the opposite? Trained to be a "good" child?

Tell each other about one of the worst experiences of your life and what you learned or gained from it. Take your time. Let each person finish before anyone else starts their story.

Chapter 15

Career Choice, Career Change

Are you ready for your second, third, or fourth career?

Do you start your workday with enthusiasm?

Are you getting paid for what you love to do?

Have you found your vocation?

Do your job skills match the needs of today's work world?

Do you know what the word *vocation* means? It means to find a life's work that *calls* to you.

Finding a career that is right for you can take time. Some people have three or four careers during their lives. Until you find a career that calls to you, you may feel dissatisfied, uncertain, and lost. These are common feelings. Many people have them.

Would you like to discover work that satisfies you? Brings excitement? Challenges your potential? Lets you start each day with happy expectations? Allows the life-style you desire? Fine. Career counselors have many ways to help you discover an exciting new career path.

To begin your vocational discovery process you need to look at your personal values and interests. Clarify what you want from life and look at the job market. Finding a match between what you enjoy doing and what needs doing is the solution.

Values Change

Adult students know they have many skills such as maintaining a home, working on an assembly line or in a restaurant, and changing the oil in a car. But what is it that you choose to spend your life energies on for the next 10 to 20 years? To start to answer this question, you must examine what you value in life. The older you get, the more your career decisions will be based on your values.

Some of the values people bring to work are:
- Helping people or making the world a better place.
- Being the boss, having power, influence over others.
- Having security, work well understood, steady paycheck.
- Having excitement, challenge, and pressure.
- Making money enough to live "the good life."
- Being allowed to choose own time, work, standards.
- Bringing beauty, variety, new ideas into the world.

Other satisfactions in your work other than money include:

- Working with things or information rather than people.
- Being in a nice place, wearing good clothes.
- Having physical activity and working out-of-doors.
- Working as a member of a friendly team.
- Performing a service of value to others.

Now take a moment to reflect on jobs you have had in the past. What were the qualities you really liked or valued? What were the things you could do without? Remember, there is no such thing as a perfect job.

Your values change a great deal with various life cycles and changes of circumstances. A man of 50, who has been bumped from the middle management of the company to which he has devoted 25 years, will feel differently than he did starting a career. It may be that loyalty to the company is now less important than being loyal to one's profession. For a woman who loses her partner and her financial security at the same time, security may be her highest value as she struggles to survive.

Transferable Skills

Every person has many skills. You may be good at communication, juggling figures, fixing things with your hands, or being sensitive to people's needs. First identify what skills you have. Let your friends help. Then decide which skills you would like to use or emphasize in your next career.

Some skills that employers value the most are:

Budget management	Supervising
Handling deadline pressure	Interviewing
Negotiating/arbitrating	Communicating
Getting along with people	Public relations
Information gathering	Instructing

More important than knowing what the working world wants is knowing what you want. You can see that the journey to a new career starts inward when you question, "What do I value in life? What have I got to offer? Which skills do I choose to use in my next career?" No one can really answer these questions for you, but various assessing methods can help sift and clarify values, skills, and interests.

Some Vocational Assessment Instruments

The following are available at most college testing departments.

Strong-Campbell Interest Inventory (SCII)

An occupational interest inventory comparing students' answering patterns with those of people satisfactorily employed in various occupations. Questions deal with likes/dislikes; norms based on a population of four-year degree, professional employees. Probably more suited to students with interest in professional fields requiring at least a four-year degree.

Career Assessment Inventory (CAI)

Similar in format to the Strong-Campbell. Normed on general population. Usually more suitable for students in vocational education.

Self-Directed Search (SDS)

A self-evaluating, less formal inventory written by John Holland. Categories cover areas of interest and competencies.

Discover

A complete, computerized, career planning system. The nine step sequence covers all aspects of career planning with an emphasis on a graphic/visual approach.

Minnesota Importance Questionnaire (MIQ)

A vocational inventory in which test takers are asked to rank job statements, thus identifying features important in their ideal job. Assists in prioritizing values and predicting job satisfaction.

California Occupational Preference System (COPS)

A self-administered and self-scored inventory, comparing relative strength of interest in many different occupations. Provides printouts of college majors. Available for different reading levels.

Myers-Briggs Type Indicator, Edwards Personal Preference Schedule, Personality Research Form (PRF)

These are personality profiles, indicating personality types. They help to understand how students perceive information and life.

Personality Mosaic

Inventory from which a student can obtain a Holland Code (as in Strong-Campbell, etc.) and a "data/people/things" rating.

Please Understand Me
(Jefferson Software)

Results are similar to the Myers-Briggs Personality Profile. Can be completed on a computer, or with pencil and paper. Used primarily as self-awareness tool.

Study Skills: Self-Exploration in Series 3
(Educational Media Corp.)

Software which identifies learning style and improves study efforts.

System of Interactive Guidance and Instructions (SIGI)

Computerized occupational assessment and exploration system in nine steps. Usually first section can be completed in approximately two hours. This system has in-depth research potential including values clarification and résumé help.

Résumé Writer II (among other software available for your personal computer)
(Career Development Software, Inc.)

A step by step approach for creating a résumé. IBM and Macintosh compatible.

What Are Your Fun Interests?

People's values change, but certain traits of personality stay the same. What do you know about your own nature?

Do you like to be left alone while you work with your hands or at something mentally challenging? Are you spurred on when you have a chance to lead others?

Do you like work where you can enjoy being around people and feel more alive when you work as a team member? What do you do in your spare time that is fun? In the spaces following write down what you know about yourself:

A Self-Assessment

My top work values:

_____

_____

_____

My top job satisfiers (other than money):

_____

_____

_____

The transferable skills I want to use on my next job:

_____

_____

_____

My fun interests are:

_____

_____

_____

Occupations that might be a good match for me are:

_____

_____

_____

Now that you have looked at who you are and what you want, it is time to examine possible careers. It is useful to have three or four careers in mind as a matter of comparison. If you do not know of someone who has that career, ask job placement, counseling/career department or an instructor in that field to help you identify a resource person for an information interview.

The three most important rules for getting job information are:

1. *Talk* to people!
2. Talk to *people*!!
3. *Talk to people*!!!

How to Get First-Hand Career Information

Job market information changes so rapidly that by the time it gets into books, it is often two years old and out of date. Magazines and computerized information systems have more current data about careers. For the most up-to-date word on occupations, there is no better way than to talk to people. A general feel for the wide market flow can be obtained in casual contacts with people and from conducting self-arranged information visits.

Guidelines for Information Interviewing

- Arrange to visit a work place where people are doing the kinds of jobs you have an interest in.
- *Never* ask for a job. An information interview is not a job interview.
- You can go by yourself or with a small group.
- Wear comfortable shoes; you may be given a tour.
- Dress to create a professional appearance: clean, well-groomed, classic.
- Do not walk around or snoop where you are not wanted.
- Come prepared to take notes; be a good reporter; get the facts.
- Stay within your prearranged timelines of 30 to 60 minutes.
- Ask only those questions that are of most importance to you.
- Make sure you know the name and title of the person you are interviewing.
- Be a good listener.

- Take a real interest in the person, the field, and the organization.
- Volunteer information about your interests, experience, and goals.
- Ask if you can stay in contact with the person.
- Always get referrals of other people to whom you may talk.
- *Always* send a thank you note.

Questions to Ask Regarding the Career
- What are the training/degree requirements for this line of work?
- What is the best way to enter this field to ensure advancement?
- Which entry-level jobs are best for learning as much as possible?
- What is the starting salary for a person in this field?
- Are there extra social/professional obligations that go with this work (unions, professional organization meetings, etc.)?
- What sort of changes are happening in this occupation that will affect future opportunities?
- Who are some people I should talk with to learn more about this career?
- Are there any special considerations for women/men starting in this field?
- Do you need special tools or equipment in this field?
- Are there any occupational hazards in this line of work?

Career Opportunities

You have started the journey inward, looking at what is true for you. You have examined values, satisfiers, skills interests and career options. Now it is time to explore the day-to-day work world and eventually hitch your wagon to the future.

Sources of current information about career opportunities, national and local, include:

- Newspapers: *Wall Street Journal, New York Times*
- Weekly news magazines: *U.S. News & World Report, Business Week*
- Monthly magazines: *Fortune, Money*
- *Vocational Biographies, Inc.* contains personal biographies of careers from skilled labor to highest professional level. Particularly useful because of data on newest careers.
- Business section of newspapers
- In-house papers and newsletters for employees
- Chamber of commerce publications
- Local magazines
- Professional and trade journals
- Civil service offices
- *Occupational Outlook Handbook* and *CIS Occupational Information* give predictions of the labor market.

> ⫸ Note: The classified section of a newspaper lists *less than 20%* of the available jobs. Use it to survey the job market for shortages of employees in certain fields, not for a comprehensive job information.

Pay Attention to Future Trends

No crystal-ball gazer can guarantee job security in the decades ahead. Changes in population, energy sources, technology, environment, and social values lead to declines in some occupations, increases in other occupations, and the birth of new occupations.

We no longer have a local/national economy. Now it is a global/outer space economy that will require cooperation and communication like never before.

The present shift from a manufacturing society to an information society will be more drastic than our shift from horse and buggy to the assembly line. Our increasing population will see people living in parts of the world presently considered uninhabitable. The lengthening life span will lead to major social changes.

No matter how carefully we study the trends of the future, there will be some occurrences, inventions, and surprises that are totally unpredictable, will affect your life profoundly, and will take a great deal of flexibility and adaptability on your part. Nourishing that part of you that looks on change as exciting and rewarding will pay big dividends. Be a survivor! The average person will change careers three to five times.

The world's population will double in 35 years. Energy consumed in the last 100 years equals one-half of all the energy consumed in the last 2,000 years. Computer related jobs will grow by 30,000 every year. There will be 17,000 more engineering positions than people to fill them. Medical workers will see big increases in the years ahead and two-thirds of American workers will be employed in services.

Retraining and educational benefits will become as important to employees as wages. More women will combine career and home interests, resulting in increased need for child-care services. On-site child care will be a top priority benefit. Seventeen percent of all workers will be in the health or education field, and there will be jobs in the health, energy, and information industries that do not yet exist. By the year 2000 only 8% of the jobs will be in manufacturing; 90% will be in services.

The new business person, with good ideas and the energy to implement them, will have great opportunity in the future. Trade with Europe, Africa, the Pacific Rim, and Spanish-speaking countries will increase.

No crystal ball can guarantee a path to job security. We can, however, make ourselves highly valued employees by being ready for change by continued education. American businesses spend billions of dollars to educate and train their employees. Seeking new opportunities to learn, getting excited over new ideas, and welcoming a chance for more training will be among the most valued traits of an employee. The thing we know for sure about the future and careers is it will bring change and challenge.

For Further Information

For further information and materials on obtaining career information and the information interview, see the list of recommended books in Resources and Selected Reading, p. 174-75.

Blazing New Trails

As you look for a new career, remember that you are a pioneer. A few years ago people did not change careers. They stayed in the same jobs all their lives, even when they felt dissatisfied and bored.

The working world has changed dramatically in recent years. According to William Bridges, a well-known transitions expert, the largest private employer in the United States is a company that provides temporary employees. Are you prepared to consider a career as a "Temp"?

In any case, you are on an exciting new adventure. The lack of clear direction about what to do is an opportunity, not a stumbling block. Searching for a second or third career, starting a first career after raising a family, is a new development for working people.

You are cutting a new path into new territory. Help and resources are available; career development and life planning classes are very valuable. But finding a satisfying vocation is up to you. So dream about a future that appeals to you and go for it!

Action Review

❏ Can you now describe your top interests, values, and skills?

❏ Have you talked with people about careers that interest you?

❏ Do you feel confident that your career choice reflects the kind of person you are?

❏ Have you investigated some recent career trends so that your choice of coursework will begin to prepare you for future developments?

Study Buddy Activity

Compare your answers to the questions about your values, interests, skills, and enjoyable activities.

Talk with each other about how much your career direction feels like a true vocation. If it doesn't, why not?

Talk about creative ways to get paid for doing what you love. Is it necessary to work for an employer? Many people, for example, are using their skills to start home businesses. Make suggestions to each other about what possibilities to explore.

Resources and Selected Reading

Chapter 1

Sher, Barbara, and Annie Gottlieb. *Teamworks!* New York: Warner Books, 1991. Contains valuable guidelines for forming and running a support group.

Chapter 2

Bob DePrato quote from *Your Hidden Credentials,* by Peter Smith. Washington, DC: Acropolis Books, 1986, p. 67. An encouraging book for adult students.

Eva Corazon Fernando-Lumba quote from *The Oregonian,* May 30, 1991.

Chapter 3

Ekstrom, Ruth B.; Abigail M. Harris; and Marlaine E. Lockheed. *How to Get College Credit for What You Have Learned as a Homemaker and Volunteer.* Princeton, NJ: Educational Testing Service.

Ronald E. Lemay story in *The Christian Science Monitor,* April 24, 1987. Center section.

Foundation Center. *Grants for Minorities.* New York: Foundation Center, 1990.

To read more about Carol Sasaki, see "From Welfare to Work Force" by Chris Phillips in *Family Circle,* Oct. 11, 1988.

Article about Gerald Winterlin, "We're Not Bums," appeared in *Parade Magazine,* May 13, 1991, p. 8.

U. S. Department of Education. *The Student Guide,* 1991.

Hechinger, Grace. "Will Your Company Pay for Your Classes?" *Glamour Magazine*, Feb. 1987.

A good book on sources of money for adult students is *Paying for Your Education: A Guide for Adult Learners*. Copies may be purchased from College Board Publication Orders, P.O. Box 2815, Princeton, NJ 08541.

Chapter 5
Edna Mae Pitman quote from *The Oregonian*, Jan. 1989.

Chapter 6
Lakein, Alan. *How to Get Control of Your Time and Your Life*. New York: New American Library, 1973. A classic in the field. Lakein shows how to establish priorities for yourself, choose activities that are of highest value to you, and minimize the amount of time you put into low payoff activities. If your school has an audiovisual library, it may have a copy of the film based on this book. You can arrange to preview the film. Take a few friends.

Slavin, Robert; N. Madden; N. Karweit; L. Dolan; B. Wasik; A. Shaw; K. Mainzer; and B. Harb. "Never Streaming: Prevention and Early Interventions Alternative to Special Education." *Journal of Learning Disabilities*. June/July 1991, pp. 373-378.

Shulman, Steven. "Facing the Invisible Handicap." *Psychology Today*, Feb. 1986.

Chapter 7
McKeachie, Wilbert J.; Donald Pollie; and Joseph Speisman. "Relieving Anxiety in Classroom Examination." *Journal of Abnormal and Social Psychology*. Vol. 50, No. 1, Jan. 1955, pp. 93-98.

Chapter 8
Strunk, William, Jr., and E. B. White. *The Elements of Style*. New York: Macmillan, 1972. This book can be valuable to anyone wanting to improve the quality and clarity of written communications. It shows how to use good grammar, punctuate correctly, and write clearly. Note: There is now a computer software program available to help check spelling and grammar.

Chapter 9

Chapman, Elwood N. *Your Attitude Is Showing.* Chicago: Science Research Associates, Inc., an IBM company, 1987.

Keirsey, David, and Marilyn Bates. *Please Understand Me.* Del Mar: Prometheus Nemesis Book Co., 1984.

Brown, Virginia, and David DeCoster. "The Myers-Briggs Type Indicator as a Developmental Measure: Implications for Student Learners in Higher Education." *Journal of College Student Development,* July 1991.

Hays, Pamela and R. Ellis. *Communication Activities for Personal Life Strategies.* Dubuque, Iowa: Kendall/Hunt Publishing Company, 1989.

Chapter 10

Mendelsohn, Pam. *Happier by Degrees.* New York: Dutton, 1980. A practical book for women in college who have families. Includes case histories of women who went back to school. Covers such topics as: how student mothers become better mothers; how husbands and children react and think; juggling roles; being a single parent; and advice from husbands of reentry students to other husbands.

Bateson, Mary Catherine. *Composing a Life.* New York: Penguin Books, 1990. This inspirational book is about "Life as a work in progress—the improvisations of five extraordinary women."

Chapter 11

Eurich, Neil. *Corporate Classrooms: The Learning Business.* Princeton, NJ: Princeton University Press, 1985.

Conroy, Mary. "Co-operative Education: Learn-and-Earn College Programs." *Better Homes & Gardens,* May 1987.

Eliason, Carol. "Co-op Can Make a Difference to Fledgling Entrepreneurs." *Workplace Education,* Sept.-Oct. 1984.

Chapter 12

Barringer, F., "Changing Picture of Metropolitan America," *The New York Times,* Aug. 1, 1992.

Brookfield, Stephen, *The Skillful Teacher*, Jossey-Bass Inc., Publishers, 1990.

"Diversity in the U.S. College Population," *Chronicle of Higher Education*, Mar.18, 1992.

Naisbitt, John, *Megatrends Asia*, Simon and Schuster. New York, 1996.

Petersen, Robert, "The Community College Vision Sees Potential in Us All," *Community College Week*, October 24, 1994.

Roueche, J. and S. Roueche. *Between a Rock and a Hard Place*, The American Association of Community Colleges, Washington, D.C., 1993.

Chapter 13

Colgrove, Melba, Ph.D., Harold Bloomfield, M.D., and Peter McWilliams. *How to Survive the Loss of Love*, Los Angeles: Prelude Press, 1976, 1991.

Flach, Frederic. *Resilience: Discovering A New Strength at Times of Stress*. New York: Fawcett Columbine, 1988.

Siebert, Al. *The Survivor Personality*, Berkeley/Perigee, New York, 1996.

Chapter 14

This chapter is adapted from *The Survivor Personality*, by Al Siebert. Berkeley/Perigee, New York, 1996, and was first published on Siebert's THRIVE*net* internet site at: http://www.thrivenet.com/.

Kipplinger Washington Letter, April 19, 1996, "unskilled workers are plentiful. Employers are looking for people who are willing to learn, can handle basic math, understand instructions, and deal well with others, especially customers and their fellow workers."

Developing a 21st Century Mind by Marsha Sinitar. New York: Villard Books, 1991. A good book on how to be creatively adaptive.

Rowan, Roy. *The Intuitive Manager*. Boston, Toronto: Little, Brown, 1986.

Getting Past No by William Ury. New York: Bantam Books, 1991. A practical book on how to develop empathy for opponents.

Merriam, Sharon B. *Learning in Adulthood*. San Francisco: Jossey-Bass, 1991.

Chapter 15

Bridges, William. *Transitions: Making Sense of Life's Changes*, Addison-Wesley, 1980.

Knoke, William. *Bold new World: The Essential Road Map to the Twenty-First Century*. Kodansha International, 1996.

Porcino, Jane. *Growing Older, Getting Better: A Handbook for Women in the Second Half of Life*. Reading, MA: Addison-Wesley, 1983.

Riley, Mary. *Corporage Healing*. Health Communication, Inc. 1960.

Tieger, Paul and Barbara Barron-Tieger. *Do What You Are* . Little, Brown and Company, 1992.

Witt, Melanie Astaire. *Job Strategies for People With Disabilities*. Peterson's Guides, 1992.

Career Opportunity News by Garrett Park Press

Kennedy, Joyce. *Joyce Lain Kennedy's Career Book*, V.G.M. Career Horizon, 1990.

Employability in High Performance Economy by Sheckley, Lamdin, Keeton.

For Further Career Search Information:

Bernard Haldane Associates Job & Career Building by Richard Germann.

Coming Alive From Nine To Five by Betty Michelozzi.

The Complete Job Search Handbook by Howard Figler.

Go Hire Yourself an Employer by Richard Irish.

Job Hunting by Charlie Mitchell and Lauren Collins.

Megatrends 2000 by John Naisbitt and Patricia Aburdene.

Mid-Career Crisis by Jean Russell Nave and Louise M. Nelson.

Want a New, Better, Fantastic Job? by Pam Gross and Peter Paskill.

What Color Is Your Parachute? by Richard Bolles.

Who's Hiring Who by Richard Lathrop.

Megatrends for Women by Patricia Aburdene and John Naisbett.

On-line Resouces

The following internet sites provide a range of useful information for college students. Most of what is listed are not-for-profit organizations. We did include some commercial listings as we found the information they contained useful and accessible. Check the sites periodically for new links. These sites are on the World Wide Web, but some have gopher access:

US Dept of Education:
http://www.ed.gov/index.html

College Board Online:
http://www.collegeboard.org/index.html

Office of Adult Learning Services (College Board Online):
http://www.collegeboard.org/offals/html/indx001.html

Adult Student Survival Guide, (The Academia Group):
http://www.mindspring.com/~academia/start.htm

ERIC Online (Educational Resources Information Center):
http://www.aspensys.com/eric/

Alternative Higher Education Network:
http://hampshire.edu/html/cs/ahen/ahen.html

Study in the USA:
http://www.studyusa.com/

Self-Help Counseling Center, University of Buffalo:
http://wings.buffalo.edu/student-life/ccenter/

Student Survival Guide Online:
http://www.skypoint.com/subscribers/jackp/survive.html

Study Skills Self Help:
http://www.ucc.vt.edu/stdysk/stdyhlp.html

Financial Aid Resources:

US Dept of Education, financial info:
http://www.ed.gov/prog_info/SFA/StudentGuide/

fastWEB (an excellent FREE scholarship matching service):
http://www.studentservices.com/fastweb/

Financial Aid Resources:
http://ssw.ab.umd.edu/findaid.html

Scholarship Search Service Primer:
http://www.excelle.com/excelle/welcome.html

Signet Bank's College Money:
http://www.signet.com/collegemoney

Sample Searching Keywords:

adult college student, continuing education, college student, student orientation, campus counseling center, career change, study, student success, college funding, financial aid, grants, scholarships.

Index

Acknowledgements

This book is the result of the contributions of many people. We wish to express our special thanks to:

Timothy L. Walter for his many contributions to the early development of material in this book.

The instructors and counselors at Portland Community College for their encouragement, feedback, information, and suggestions.

Mary Karr for her delightful personal comments and careful proof reading.

Marcia House for her excellent professional secretarial skills.

Maris Bishoprick for keeping us current on developments in the library.

Clarice Anderson for financial aid information.

The students and instructors who critiqued the first and second editions and provided us with valuable feedback.

Teresa Rosen for her artistic skills and creativity.

George Vaterneck for many years of supportive mentoring.

Wilbert J. McKeachie and the University of Michigan psychology department faculty for creating a climate of professionalism in teaching.

John Gardner, Stuart Hunter, and the other Freshman Year Experience staff at the University of South Carolina for their dedication to first year students and their excellent stewardship.

Our families for their constant support and appreciation.

Feedback Request

Please let us know how you did! How was *The Adult Student's Guide to Survival and Success* helpful to you? How did having a success group work out?

Do you have any suggestions on how *The Adult Student's Guide* could be improved? Write to us c/o:

Practical Psychology Press
PO Box 535
Portland, OR 97207

PracPsyPrs@aol.com

http://www.thrivenet.com/press.html

Also Available

Books:

The Survivor Personality	ISBN: 0-399-52230-1
Al Siebert, Ph.D.	$12.00
Peaking Out	ISBN: 0-944227-10-4
Al Siebert as told to Sam Kimball	$19.95
Dreaming Insights: A 5-Step Plan for Discovering the	
Meaning in Your Dreams	ISBN: 0-944227-08-2
Gillian Holloway, Ph.D.	$11.95

Cassette:

Thriving in a World of Non-Stop Change
Al Siebert, Ph.D. $12.95

Please add $2.00 postage & handling for books, $1.00 for the cassette. Send check or money order to:

> **Practical Psychology Press**
> **PO Box 535**
> **Portland, OR 97207**
>
> **PracPsyPrs@aol.com**

Satisfaction guaranteed.

For a survivor personality self-evaluation, visit our web site at:

> **http://www.thrivenet.com/**